NATIONAL CONVENTIONS

Nominations Under the Big Top

JAMES W. DAVIS, Chairman Political Science Department
Central Michigan University
Mount Pleasant, Michigan

Politics in Government Series
Mary Earhart Dillon, Editor

BARRON'S EDUCATIONAL

SERIES, INC.

WOODBURY, NEW YORK

All inquiries should be addressed to:
   Barron's Educational Series, Inc.
   113 Crossways Park Drive
   Woodbury, New York 11797

Library of Congress Catalog Card No. 77–189866
International Standard Book No. 0–8120–0443–4

PRINTED IN THE UNITED STATES OF AMERICA

CONTENTS ★

5 **The National Nominating Convention Under Attack**   **67**

6 **National Convention Reform**   **84**

TABLES

TITLES IN THIS SERIES

General Editor: Mary Earhart Dillon, formerly Chairman of the Department of Political Science, Queens College of the City University of New York

INTRODUCTION ★

The Politics of Government Series is a continuing publication of paperbacks by distinguished scholars on controversial political and social issues of "here and now." These pamphlets provide students of current American problems with ready and valid technical aid as source material for discussions, reports, term papers, speeches, and debates. Invaluable are the 100 appropriate topics in each pamphlet from which the student may more easily prepare his class assignment, and also a recent bibliography.

The National Conventions: Nominations Under the Big Top by James W. Davis is an enlightened discussion of the action and the problem of choosing the presidential candidates. The convention system has been laughed at abroad and scoffed at by intellectuals at home. Many ask if this is the best way for people to select candidates for the highest office in the land. Is it an open means of participation for all groups, and is the procedure so bawdy as to prevent the sober choice of worthy men? The problem is representation and procedure. The McGovern plan of reform is well explained, and the author also gives his own ideas for change. As to procedure, he describes the organization and work of the convention which leads finally to the exciting moment of nomination. At the same time, he gives a glowing account of the fanfare and color of the big show, adopted largely from the county fairs of a century and more ago. He flavors the music, singing, cavorting, and politicking that has made the convention a unique institution in American politics—indeed, a tradition, a part of Americana.

Professor Davis is a recognized scholar in the field of politics and elections. He has participated as an official delegate in many national and state party conventions. Further, he has engaged in political campaigns in Minnesota and Michigan. In fact, he is a veteran of the hustings and hence knows politics from the inside. He has published the well-known book *Presi-*

dential Primaries: Road to the White House as well as articles in learned journals. The author took his doctorate at the University of Minnesota. After beginning his academic career as the Principal of the North Dakota High Schools, he did a stint in Washington as an administrative official in the Department of Defense. Returning to academe he taught at Washington State University and Saint Cloud State College before joining the faculty at Central Michigan University where he is chairman of the Department of Political Science.

JAMES W. DAVIS
Central Michigan University

EMERGENCE OF A
NATIONAL CONVENTION
SYSTEM

No American institutions so fascinate and so appall the citizenry of the Republic (and so absolutely flabbergast foreigners) as do those vulgar, those quarrelsome, those unspeakably chaotic rites by which U.S. political parties choose candidates for the Presidency. The quadriennial conventions assume the loftiest of partisan obligations; but no other such convocations anywhere in the civilized world perform their functions amid such torrents of hoarse and lamentable oratory, such displays of hypocritical bedlam and such bare-faced recourse to the mores of the poker table and floa market. They are motivated by an arrant opportunism, will seize upon a Warren Harding as ecstatically as upon an Abraham Lincoln, and are such natural incubators of pathos and low comedy that their functionaries sometimes seem to be engaged in some large-scale revival of 19th century burlesque.[1]

The quotation above explains, in large part, why the national nominating conventions are "as American as cherry pie." Indeed, the national conventions are beyond doubt one of the most unique and eminently practical political institutions ever devised by American party leaders. How else, barring a national primary system, could a huge federal Republic of fifty states develop another political instrument that provides relatively equal representation to rank-and-file party members in all 435 congressional districts that encompass 3,000 plus counties, 10,-000 cities and smaller municipalities, and hundreds of townships and rural precincts? The answer to this question almost defies a solution. It seems fair to conclude that party leaders, if they had not developed the national nominating convention, would have had to invent it. What other political organ could better serve the variegated interests in each major party and accomplish the following objectives in choosing a national leader: (1) provide for the diversity of representation, (2) possess the flexibility to reconcile deep factional cleavages within a party, (3) produce a binding nomination acceptable to virtually all elements within the party, and (4) select nominees who possess strong likelihood of winning voter support.

Clearly, the national nominating conventions have also served the nation well. The conventions have aided in the preservation of the two-party system; helped foster vigorous competition between the parties; and systematically excluded extremists from winning the nomination and thereby facilitated the maintenance of a democratic consensus within the country. Though undreamed of when the United States Constitution was drafted, the national conventions have come to occupy a crucial role in the leadership selection process for the highest office in the land—the President of the United States. Certainly the political machinery that selects candidates for the office that is commonly regarded as the most powerful in the Free World deserves close study. This will be the topic of this monograph.

Nominations by Congressional Caucus

The national nominating convention did not develop overnight. Instead, it evolved slowly in the second quarter of the nineteenth century. Until 1824 nominations for President were made by Congressional party caucuses, that is, the party leadership on Capitol Hill. But in President James Monroe's final year of office, a battle royal for the nomination developed among his potential successors—Andrew Jackson, John Quincy Adams, Henry Clay and William Crawford. The Congressional Caucus was unable to agree on a nominee, though a "rump" session gave the nod to William Crawford, Secretary of the Treasury in Monroe's Cabinet. Andrew Jackson and his political lieutenants knew that in the four-man race they did not have enough votes in the Atlantic Seaboard-dominated Congressional Caucus to gain the nomination; so the Jacksonians boycotted the caucus. Instead, Jackson was nominated by the Tennessee legislature and those of several other states. Jackson received more electoral votes than his rivals, but he did not have a majority of the Electoral College as required by the Constitution. He lost the election when the House of Representatives chose John Quincy Adams as President. However, the bitter Jacksonian protests following his defeat helped dethrone "King Caucus."

In 1827, Senator Martin Van Buren, leader of the Jacksonian forces on Capitol Hill, proposed that a national nominating convention be called to nominate candidates for President.[2] No immediate action, however, was taken on this proposal. For the moment it was unnecessary, for the Tennessee legislature had already renominated Jackson, who in the meantime had resigned from the U.S. Senate to commence campaigning. In 1828, President Adams was renominated by a National Republican state party convention in Maine, later endorsed by state conventions in New York and Pennsylvania and the legislatures of Vermont and Massachusetts.

The Transitional Period

During the transition from the congressional caucus system to the national nominating convention, which became firmly established by the 1840's, at least four methods for nominating the president were used. The most popular method of presidential nomination was by state legislative caucus, for example, a joint meeting of both houses of a state legislature.[3] The second method used to nominate presidential candidates in the states during the transitional period was by the "mixed" convention, composed of the party members of the legislature and delegates from those counties and towns not represented in the legislature by members to the party holding the conclave. Indeed, this method of nominating a presidential candidate carried over to the early period of the national convention. According to Dallinger, a nineteenth century authority on nominations:

> . . . in February 1843, a convention composed of the Whig members of the Virginia Legislature, and of two hundred delegates from different parts of the state, was held at Richmond at which resolutions were adopted nominating Henry Clay as the Whig candidate for the Presidency, and referring the nomi-

nation of a candidate for the Vice Presidency to the national convention.[4]

Third, state conventions, as indicated earlier, were also used to nominate presidential candidates during the interim period. In some states the party continued to "nominate" presidential candidates—the action serving merely to reflect party sentiment within the state.[5] Fourth, in other states it was a common practice to obtain the presidential preferences of rank-and-file voters at various types of public meetings. Throughout the country mass meetings were held, at which formal resolutions nominating a candidate for president were adopted. These various meetings were, in effect, gatherings to ratify the nomination of candidates who had been previously nominated by state conventions or legislative caucuses. Today we would term these meetings party rallies, though these early meetings formally adopted nominating resolutions.[6]

None of the four nominating methods sketched above met the needs of the emerging party system in the young, sprawling Republic. Indeed, it is entirely possible that if the state convention or legislative caucus system had persisted, a multi-party system might have evolved, since each state conclave was completely free to put forward any candidate that captured its fancy. That this patchwork system did not have many vocal advocates facilitated the emergence of the national nominating convention, in which delegates from all states of the Union would meet under one roof to select a presidential and vice presidential candidate. The fact that party conventions had been used on the county and state level in most states for more than two decades before the first national convention was held undoubtedly facilitated the transition from earlier nominating procedures to the national convention system.

Evolution of National Convention

Jackson's spectacular victory in 1828 signaled the emergence of a highly-organized political movement based upon mass support rather than congressional political power. The effects of this popular movement soon were to be reflected in the new machinery for nominating Presidents—the national convention. The first national nominating convention was convened, not by the Jacksonians, but by the short-lived Anti-masonic party in 1831. At this Baltimore convention, which 116 delegates from 13 states attended, the Antimasons nominated William Wirt (President Monroe's Attorney General) for the Presidency. The Antimasons, who lacked representation in Congress and elsewhere, sought to use the convention as a means for generating national support. Though the Antimasons did not survive to hold another convention, this minor party established four precedents that have influenced major party conventions and national party organization ever since:

1. Delegations were chosen in a manner determined by each state.
2. Each state was entitled to as many votes as the state's representation in Congress.
3. A special majority—the Antimasons had decreed three-fourths of the delegates—was required for nomination.
4. An Antimasonic national committee was appointed to carry on national party business between elections.[7]

The second national convention was called by the National Republicans in December 1831. Since this party, which had supported President John Quincy Adams' reelection bid in 1828, had so few members in Congress, the party needed a mechanism to give it a semblance of nationwide representation. The National Republican convention nominated Henry Clay for President and John Sergeant, his running-mate. But with Clay's overwhelming defeat in 1832, these former Federalists and dissident elements of the Democratic-Republicans (the original name of the Jacksonian Democrats) abandoned future efforts to keep the party alive.

Jackson's supporters were next to call for a national convention, held in May 1832, in Baltimore. The purpose of the Democratic Convention was not to assure Jackson's renomination, since this was a foregone conclusion. Instead, the chief reason for utilizing this new mechanism was to help heal the bitter split in the Administration over the vice presidential candidacy between the incumbent Vice President John C. Calhoun and Secretary of State Martin Van Buren, the eventual nominee. One of Jackson's advisers felt a national convention would help pull the party together by drawing on Jackson's vast popularity. Also, the timing of the convention after Congress had adjourned was aimed "to prevent an improper interference by members of Congress."[8] Overall, the national convention system was launched by three parties for the 1832 campaign as an instrument for developing party representation independent of Congress.

With the newly-emerging party system in a state of flux, the authority of the national party conventions to determine presidential nominations was not accorded full recognition until the 1840 campaign. After the Democrats held a second national convention in 1835 and a third in 1839, and the newly-formed Whig party used a national convention in 1839 to select its candidate— William Henry Harrison—for its 1840 campaign, the national nominating convention became a permanent element of the American party system. Indeed, the national conventions have become one of the most durable political institutions in the Western world. National conventions have been held by the major parties quadrennially—in peace time or war—ever since 1840.

By 1848, the national nominating convention had become completely divorced from the congressional party for choosing presidential candidates. The year 1848 marked the last time the Democratic Congressional Caucus issued the "call" for the Democratic convention; four years later, the Whig congressional caucus also performed this function for the last time. Henceforth, the presidential branch of each national party asserted its complete independence of congressional influence.

Without question the national nominating convention was well suited for the young nation because:

1. It was representative in character;
2. It divorced presidential nominations from congressional control;
3. It provided for a broad-based formulation of a party program;
4. It concentrated the party's strength behind a single presidential ticket;
5. It reconciled personal rivalries and group or sectional interests.[9]

Before the convention system emerged, no caucus of the party leaders in Congress could adequately represent all party elements or areas of the country. The problem of how to achieve representation in a congressional district held by the opposition party had never been resolved. In contrast, the party convention provided delegate representation, no matter which party controlled office, for all party constituencies—the congressional districts, the cities, the small towns, the rural areas. The convention also provided voting rights for elected officeholders—senators, governors, congressmen, and state legislators—as well as party officials and rank-and-file delegates. In short, the national convention, as its name implies, served as an instrument to give representation nationwide to all constituencies within both major parties.

Functions Performed by National Conventions

Although the Civil War temporarily upset the operation of the two-party system, the national conventions continued uninterruptedly after the bloody conflict and have remained essentially unchanged for more than a century. Throughout this period the national convention has performed four major functions for the parties:

1. Nominated Presidential and Vice Presidential candidates acceptable to most factions within the party, except in 1860 and 1912.

2. Hammered out party platforms. This function evolved from
   the earlier occasional practice of presenting "an address to
   the people." Early platform-making was usually deferred
   until after the nominations had been completed. But in 1852
   the parties sought to help reconcile party fissures by adopt-
   ing the platform before selecting presidential candidates.
   This order of the agenda has prevailed, with few exceptions, to the present.
3. Served as the campaign rally mechanism for the national
   party. This function has continued to take on greater importance, especially in recent decades. From the beginning the
   conventions were held as public meetings. Thus, although
   the campaign function was not explicitly recognized, the
   publicity and rallying activities of conventions have always
   been an integral part of these huge party conclaves.
4. Served as the governing-body of the national party. This
   activity, which is exemplified by the election of a continuing national committee each four years, has been an integral part of national conventions since the 1850's. The federal nature of the American party system was always
   formally recognized by giving equal representation (two
   members—one man and one woman) to each state, until the
   GOP gave additional representation to states with pro-
   Republican majorities. Before every national convention
   the national committee prescribes the number of delegates
   allocated to each state, establishes the convention rules, ap-
   points the chairman of the various convention committees—credentials, rules, resolutions, and platform—and
   handles all arrangements for the quadrennial conclave.

As already indicated, the national nominating conventions
have operated with essentially the same format over the years—
but with one major exception. The spread of the presidential
primary system to more than half the states of the Union during
the period 1900–1918 modified the delegate selection process by
giving rank-and-file voters the right to express a preference on
national convention delegates or to register a personal choice for
President in the primary. The introduction of the presidential
primaries "opened up" the nominating process to more popular

influence and pressure, without depriving the party's national convention of its ultimate prerogative of picking its presidential nominee. More will be said about presidential primaries later in this study. Let's now turn to an examination of the convention machinery and its operation.

CONVENTION MACHINERY AND ORGANIZATION

$\mathcal{2}$ ★ ★ ★

For delegates of the out-party the national convention is the culmination of four long years of waiting to get another chance to nominate and, hopefully, elect the party's nominee to the highest office in the land. But conventions simply do not automatically happen. Extensive planning is required to mount these quadriennial extravaganzas. Let's take a moment to look into the planning that must be done before the temporary chairman of the convention pounds the gavel and announces: "The Delegates will please come to order . . . ."

Convention Planning

The task of planning the next national convention, as indicated in the last chapter, belongs to the party's national committee. More than a year in advance of the national convention, a sub-committee search team explores the invitations and offers to hold the convention from several cities. For 1972 the Democratic national committee chose Miami Beach, Florida—site of the 1968 Republican conclave. San Diego, California was selected for the 1972 GOP conclave—because it was reportedly the personal preference of President Nixon, whose summer home at San Clemente is only a 55-mile drive from the convention site.

For the out-party various financial and organizational considerations are weighed before the convention choice is made. In the fall of 1967, for example, Miami Beach officials offered the Republican National Committee $850,000 (a new high) to hold their convention on the sun-drenched shores of Biscayne Bay. A few weeks later, Mayor Richard J. Daley and his businessmen associates topped Miami Beach's financial bid by offering the Democrats just under $1 million to hold their national convention in the Windy City. The television network executives pleaded with the Democrats to hold their convention in Miami Beach, too, so that the networks could avoid a second costly equipment and personnel move. But Mayor Daley's influence with incumbent President Johnson, who agreed on Chicago as the convention site, triumphed over the network executives' pleas. The massive anti-war demonstrations and brutal police counteraction that produced a brawling, divided party were not, of course, anticipated when President Johnson and the Democratic National Committee opted for Chicago.

Generally, the basic considerations in picking a convention city include the availability of several thousand hotel rooms and the facilities to "care and feed" several thousand party faithful. For the out-of-power party the chief political consideration is that the host city not be in a state that has a leading candidate for the Presidency.

For the in-party the personal wishes of the President are the deciding factor. Miami Beach, for example, was thought to be the preference of many GOP'ers for 1972, since its 20,000 hotel rooms and its controlled access from the mainland (which provides maximum security against potential demonstrators) made it a prime site for the GOP. As a matter of fact, the city fathers of San Diego had formally decided earlier that it had no interest in either the Republican and Democratic convention because of the cost and the strain that would be placed on the municipal services. However, after White House representatives brought word that President Nixon was prepared to use his influence to swing the choice to San Diego, city and county officials did an about-face and hurriedly put together a $1.5 million bid.[1] Proximity alone was not the only factor that influenced the President's choice—California's 45 electoral votes that Mr. Nixon desperately needs to win reelection in 1972 weighed heavily in his preference for San Diego.

Major Convention Committees

To handle the comprehensive large-scale planning for the convention, the national committee assigns these duties to four major committees:

1 CREDENTIALS This committee is concerned with the ted-
ious work of certifying the delegates and alternates for all fifty
states and the territories. The committee also has the thankless
job of settling contests between state delegations claiming the
same seats. It must rule on all challenges against any delegate
or alternate. Unless the committee's verdicts are challenged on
the floor, their decision will be accepted on a voice vote by the
convention.

2 PERMANENT ORGANIZATION Traditionally, this committee selects the permanent officials of the convention—permanent
chairman, secretary, and the sergeant at arms.

3 RULES Customarily, this committee adopts most of the rules
and precedents followed by earlier conventions. But, occasionally, the committee has had to face a thorny question, for example, repeal of the unit rule at the 1968 Democratic convention
and repeal of the century-old "two-thirds rule" at the 1936 Democratic convention. To accommodate the television networks the
rules committee of both parties have sought, without appearing
to be arbitrary, to shorten nominating speeches and the number
of seconding speeches, the length of demonstrations (at the 1968
Democratic convention floor demonstrations were banned), and
generally to expedite convention business.[2]

4 RESOLUTIONS Platform-making is the chief function of this
committee. But the committee also drafts various resolutions
that range from thanking the host city to applauding retired
party heroes.
  Composed of prominent party leaders (two from each state),
these four committees handle this enormous amount of work
gratis, since the only salaried workers at the convention are staff
members of the national committees.[3] The national convention,
as noted by the authors of the leading study on this institution,
"Takes on some of the characteristics of an international conference of delegations from sovereign states, some of which may be

democracies, others autocracies of one sort or another."[4] All fifty states and several territories are represented at the quadriennial conclave, though not in equal numbers.

Apportionment of Delegates

The party's national committee is vested with the sole responsibility of apportioning delegates among the states. This vital decision-making has taken on additional importance in recent years as some of the minority groups, especially in the Democratic party, seek to apply the same "one-man, one vote" principle derived from the Supreme Court's reapportionment cases to the allocation of convention delegates. These groups argue that the states contributing the most votes proportionately to the national party ticket should be given additional delegate votes. More will be said in a moment about granting additional delegate vote on the basis of the one-man, one vote principle. But, first, a brief historical review of delegate apportionment is needed for background purposes.

From the beginning of the conventions system in 1832, the basic allocation of voting power to each state in both parties was the same as that of the Electoral College—the combined total of senators and representatives from each state. Before the Civil War this allocation system worked rather well, since voter support for the Democrats and Whigs was relatively evenly-divided between the two parties.

GOP APPORTIONMENT   Toward the end of the nineteenth century, however, the electoral college formula was questioned by critics, especially in the GOP, who pointed out that in "one-party" states the electoral college principle overrepresented the minority party. Thus, the southern Republican delegations were heavily overrepresented at GOP conventions. This controversy finally boiled over at the 1912 GOP convention, when Teddy Roosevelt's partisans claimed that Taft "stole" the nomination with the "postmaster vote" from the "rotten borough" southern delegations.[5] These delegates voted for Taft because their federal jobs (during this era postmasters were patronage appointees) depended upon their pro-Taft loyalty.

Following the party's disastrous defeat in 1912, the Republican National Committee (though with no formal mandate to act)

TABLE 2.1   **GOP Convention Delegate Apportionment 1968–1972**

STATE	1968	1972	1972 PRESIDENTIAL ELECTORS	STATE	1968	1972	1972 PRESIDENTIAL ELECTORS
Alabama	26	17	3	New Hampshire	8	14	4
Alaska	12	12	3	New Jersey	40	40	17
Arizona	16	18	6	New Mexico	14	14	4
Arkansas	18	18	6	New York	92	88	41
California	86	96	45	North Carolina	26	32	13
Colorado	18	20	7	North Dakota	8	12	3
Connecticut	16	22	8	Ohio	58	56	25
Delaware	12	12	3	Oklahoma	22	22	8
District of				Oregon	18	18	6
Columbia	9	9	3	Pennsylvania	64	60	27
Florida	34	40	17	Puerto Rico	5	5	—
Georgia	30	24	12	Rhode Island	14	8	4
Guam	—	3	—	South Carolina	22	22	8
Hawaii	14	14	4	South Dakota	14	14	4
Idaho	14	14	4	Tennessee	28	26	10
Illinois	58	58	26	Texas	56	52	26
Indiana	26	32	13	Utah	8	14	4
Iowa	24	22	8	Vermont	12	12	3
Kansas	20	20	7	Virginia	24	30	12
Kentucky	24	24	9	Virgin Islands	3	3	—
Louisiana	26	20	10	Washington	24	24	9
Maine	14	8	4	West Virginia	14	18	6
Maryland	26	26	10	Wisconsin	30	28	11
Massachusetts	34	34	14	Wyoming	12	12	3
Michigan	48	48	21				
Minnesota	26	26	10				
Mississippi	20	13	7	Total	1,333	1,346	538
Missouri	24	30	12	Needed to			
Montana	14	14	4	Nominate	667	674	
Nebraska	16	16	5	Needed to			
Nevada	12	12	3	Elect			270

took upon itself to give additional representation to those states —all in the North—that cast a heavy vote for the Republican party. Under the new rules adopted in 1914, one additional delegate was granted to each congressional district for each 7,500 Republican votes cast for President in 1908 (the 1912 GOP vote was not deemed a fair measure of Republican strength) or for congressman in 1914.[6] As a result of this reapportionment plan, eleven southern states lost seventy-eight delegates in 1916 and seven more in 1920; two northern states—New York and Massachusetts—dropped a total of six delegates between 1916–1920.[7]

The GOP national committee, taking into consideration the advent of women's suffrage and national population growth, raised the requirement for a second district delegate in 1924. For the first time, the GOP adopted a system of bonus delegates. Three bonus delegates were apportioned to each state carried by the GOP in the preceding presidential election—a provision benefitting northern states. Since then, the bonus delegate provisions have been expanded repeatedly. For example, the GOP convention in 1940 decreed that in 1944, a state could still have its three bonus votes, even though it failed to carry the presidential election—provided it should elect a Republican senator in the following off-year election. Four years later, the 1948 GOP convention increased the number of bonus delegates, effective 1952, for party victory in a state from three to six. Furthermore, this delegate bonus was made available retroactively for GOP success in the preceding presidential, senatorial, and gubernatorial election.[8]

With the rise of the Republican party in the South in the 1960's, the problem of overrepresentation of the South has almost disappeared. In 1968, the southern states held approximately 26.7 per cent of the national convention delegate vote (356 of 1,333 delegates), as Table 2.2 (p. 16) indicates.

DEMOCRATIC DELEGATE APPORTIONMENT   Generally, the Democrats have had less trouble than the GOP with delegate apportionment. Until 1936, the Democrats relied basically on the electoral college principle, allowing a state delegation to be twice

TABLE 2.2   **GOP Convention Strength Region-By-Region at the 1952, 1960, 1964 and 1968 Conventions**

	1952	1960	1964	1968
East	372*(30.8%)	386*(29.0%)	355*(27.1%)	355*(26.6%)
South	229 (19.0%)	329 (24.7%)	325 (24.8%)	356 (26.7%)
Midwest	372 (30.8%)	372 (28.0%)	364 (27.8%)	352 (26.4%)
West	229†(19.0%)	242 (18.2%)	256 (19.6%)	262 (19.7%)
††Totals	1,206	1,331	1,308	1,333

* Includes Washington, D.C. delegation.
† Includes Alaska and Hawaii, which were not yet states.
†† Adds in Puerto Rico and Virgin Islands to regional totals.

Source   *New York Times,* December 5, 1966.

the size of its senatorial-congressional delegation. But in 1936, as a concession to the South in connection with the repeal of the two-thirds rule, the Democratic national convention directed its national committee to recommend a plan that reflected "the Democratic strength within each state."[9] The 1940 convention, which nominated President Roosevelt for a third term, approved a new rule, effective in 1944, that granted two bonus delegates to each state that went Democratic in the last preceding presidential election. For the 1948 convention the Democratic national committee increased the bonus to four votes for states going Democratic in the preceding presidential election. Before the 1952 convention the national committee turned to another apportionment problem—the nine states faced with the loss of delegates as a result of congressional reapportionment following the 1950 census. Yielding to pressure from these states, which included New York, the Democratic national committee adopted a special rule that no state should lose convention votes by reason of congressional reapportionment. (The GOP, faced with a similar problem, took no action and left it to the individual states to adjust their delegate loss as they best saw fit.)

In preparation for the 1956 convention, the Democratic national committee broadened the use of bonus votes to give credit for gubernatorial and senatorial victories for the first time. Thus, many of the states credited with bonus delegates for 1952 were given additional bonus votes in 1956 for voting Democratic in 1952 or 1954 for President, governor, or senator. In other words, these states received a total of eight bonus votes in 1956, and a precedent was established for the accumulation of bonus votes from convention to convention.[10] In 1964, the Democratic National Committee increased the "victory bonus" to ten delegates for each state that cast its electoral votes for the Democratic presidential nominee. As a result of this generosity, Democratic conventions have been getting almost as large as a Madison Square Garden championship fight audience.

Why have the Democratic conclaves become so huge? The chief reasons are that the national committee is under heavy pressure to increase the size of state delegations. Moreover, the national committee has not wished to offend any state party by reducing the size of its delegation, even though the state party failed to carry the ticket at the last election. Over and above these considerations, delegate seats to national conventions are prized possessions among party gladiators. Consequently, the more seats available, the less likelihood that the party zealots will be passed over at convention time. Also, the desire to create a mass rally atmosphere has undoubtedly prompted the Democratic convention managers to turn the conclave into a vast theatrical for the television networks.

That party convention reform would be a priority planning item for the 1972 Democratic national convention was almost a foregone conclusion after the widespread charges by the followers of Senator Eugene McCarthy at the 1968 Chicago convention that the delegate selection process was "rigged" in favor of Vice President Humphrey and his pro-Administration supporters. Before the 1968 convention opened, a McCarthy-sponsored reform committee, headed by Governor (now Senator) Harold Hughes of Iowa, made the following charges:

1. The delegate selection process for more than 600 delegates —one-fourth of the total number of delegates—were selected without any form of direct voter participation since 1966.
2. The 110 national committeemen and national committeewomen from the 50 states and territories were elected four years before the 1968 convention, long before any of the candidates or major issues of 1968 were known.
3. In at least twenty states party professionals held whip-hand control over the selection of delegates.
4. Minority groups, women, and young voters were denied fair representation at the 1968 convention.[11]

In order to correct these abuses, Democratic National Chairman Fred Harris in 1969 appointed a special Commission of Party Structure and Delegate Selection—better known as the McGovern Commission, after its chairman, Senator George McGovern of South Dakota. The Democratic task force, after more than a year of hearings and deliberations, recommended a number of delegate selection process reforms, which will be discussed later in this monograph.[12] The task of working out an equitable system for apportioning delegates for the 1972 Democratic convention, however, was assigned to the Commission on Rules of the Democratic National Committee—better known as the O'Hara Commission, after its chairman, Congressman James G. O'Hara of Michigan.

In February 1971, the Democratic National Committee accepted a modified version of the O'Hara Commission apportionment plan for the 1972 Democratic convention. According to the O'Hara formula, each state's Democratic vote for President was to count one-half and the population of the state, one-half. The modified version finally accepted by the national party's executive committee was based on a formula computed by counting Presidential vote 46 per cent and Electoral College strength 54 per cent.[13] Table 2.3 (pp. 20–21) shows the allocation of delegates to the states at the 1968 Democratic National Convention together with the recommendation of the O'Hara Reform Commission for the 1972 convention, and the apportionment plan adopted by the Democratic National Committee at its February 1971 meeting.

Although the differences between the O'Hara Commission and the party's executive committee were not great—under the O'Hara plan the eight biggest states would have had a majority of the votes and under the other plan the nine biggest states would have had a majority—the executive committee proposal avoided severe losses for the smallest states. At the committee meeting the small states failed to put across their plan that would have based the apportionment entirely on the Electoral College. According to their chief spokesman, former Governor of Kentucky Edward T. Breathitt, the use of the Electoral College as part or all of the formula "was in keeping with the spirit of the Constitution."[14] Spokesmen for the large states preferred a formula that would have based the delegate apportionment entirely on Democratic voting strength—the "one-Democrat, one-vote" principle. In retrospect, the chief reason that the O'Hara Commission's plan was not accepted is that the National Committee is composed of two members from each state—which gives a disproportionately large voice to the small states. And since it was the smaller states whose ox was being gored by the O'Hara Commission's recommendations—the ten smallest states had 8.71 per cent of the delegates at Chicago in 1968 and the O'Hara Commission gave them only 2.80 per cent in 1972—the reform plan was voted down.

In any case, the Democratic National Committee's apportionment plan for 1972 has already come under court attack in the District of Columbia. In June 1971 a Federal district court judge invalidated the Democratic National Committee's new formula for allocating 1972 delegates among the states.[15] The challenge to the Democratic National Committee plan, brought by a coalition of Democratic reform groups and party leaders, seeks to force the National Committee to adopt a "one-Democrat, one-vote" formula, one that would base relative convention strength solely on how large a vote each state had garnered for the Democratic Presidential candidate, either in the last election or averaged over several elections. If the court's decision is upheld by

TABLE 2.3 **Democratic Delegate Apportionment 1968 and 1972 and O'Hara Commission Recommendation**

State	1968 Convention	O'Hara Commission	1972 Convention
Alabama	32	36	37
Alaska	22	4	10
Arizona	19	21	25
Arkansas	33	24	27
California	174	294	271
Colorado	35	32	36
Connecticut	44	51	51
Delaware	22	8	13
District of Columbia	23	12	15
Florida	63	83	81
Georgia	43	52	53
Hawaii	26	11	17
Idaho	25	10	17
Illinois	118	181	170
Indiana	63	79	76
Iowa	46	45	46
Kansas	38	32	35
Kentucky	46	46	47
Louisiana	36	42	44
Maine	27	16	20
Maryland	49	54	53
Massachusetts	72	107	102
Michigan	96	140	132
Minnesota	52	64	64
Mississippi	24	21	25
Missouri	69	75	73
Montana	26	11	17
Nebraska	30	21	24
Nevada	22	6	11
New Hampshire	26	12	18
New Jersey	82	115	109
New Mexico	26	14	18
New York	190	301	278
North Carolina	59	65	64
North Dakota	25	10	14
Ohio	115	163	153
Oklahoma	41	35	39
Oregon	35	32	34
Pennsylvania	130	196	182
Rhode Island	27	18	22
South Carolina	28	28	32
South Dakota	26	11	17
Tennessee	51	49	49
Texas	104	139	130

State	1968 Convention	O'Hara Commission	1972 Convention
Utah	26	15	19
Vermont	22	7	12
Virgina	54	53	53
Washington	47	53	52
West Virginia	38	32	35
Wisconsin	59	69	67
Wyoming	22	5	11
Total	2,599	3,000	3,000
Canal Zone	5	(A)	3
Guam	5	(A)	3
Puerto Rico	8	(A)	7
Virgin Islands	5	(A)	3

(A)—The Rules Commission did not submit specific numbers concerning the territories.

Source: *New York Times,* February 20, 1971.

higher courts, and the national committee is forced to adopt the "one-Democrat, one-vote" formula based on the 1968 returns, New York will go from 278 to 324 delegates, California from 271 to 311 and Massachusetts from 102 to 141. In contrast, Alabama would drop from 37 to 19, Alaska from 22 to 4, and Nevada from 22 to 6.[16]

Methods of Selecting Delegates

National convention delegates are chosen by three methods: (a) In nearly three-fifths of the states they are selected by state and district conventions; (b) In slightly more than two-fifths of the states they are chosen in presidential primary elections in which the voters choose the delegates directly and which sometimes permit the voters to express a preference on the presidential candidate of their choice. In a few primary states district delegates may be chosen by the voters and the delegates-at-large by the state convention or party committee; (c) In 1968, four states and one territory, Puerto Rico, state executive committees

TABLE 2.4   Delegate Selection Systems in 1968[1]

CONVENTION SYSTEMS		COMMITTEE SYSTEMS	PRIMARY SYSTEMS
Alaska	Missouri	Arizona	Alabama
Canal Zone	Montana	Arkansas	California
Colorado	Nevada	Georgia[2]	District of
Connecticut	New Mexico	Louisiana[2]	Columbia
Delaware	North Carolina	Maryland	Florida
Guam	North Dakota	Puerto Rico	Massachusetts
Hawaii	South Carolina	Rhode Island	Nebraska
Idaho	Tennessee		New Hampshire
Iowa	Texas		New Jersey
Kansas	Utah		Ohio
Kentucky	Vermont		Oregon
Maine	Virginia		South Dakota
Michigan	Virgin Islands		West Virginia
Minnesota	Wyoming		
Mississippi			

selected the delegates (at least in Democratic party). Two additional states, Georgia and Louisiana, permitted their Governors, in effect, to appoint their entire delegation to the national convention. Although Table 2.4 above summarizes the various methods used in 1968 to select national convention delegates in the Democratic Party, the procedures used by the GOP do not differ appreciably, although in Georgia and Louisiana Republican congressional district and state conventions picked the delegates.

PARTY CONVENTION SYSTEM   Defenders of the national convention argue that the machinery through which the party allows precinct, county, and congressional district and state convention delegates the opportunity to participate in the selection of national convention delegates permits a good deal of "grassroots" participation. Under the party convention system delegates from precinct or township constituencies are elected to county conventions which, in turn, elect delegates to congressional district and state party conventions. This system of delegates is regarded by its defenders as the essence of "participatory democracy." But the truth of the matter is that for many years party professionals—for example, state, district and county chairmen—have dominated the delegate-selection machinery in most convention states. This is why presidential aspirants try to establish and maintain ties with these party leaders in the convention states. Occasional appearances at statewide fund-raising dinners, personal visits to campaign on behalf of the senatorial, congressional, and gubernatorial candidates, and frequent correspondence with these leaders are important ways of keeping in touch with these party decision-makers. Recently, the presidential candidacies of Senator Barry Goldwater and former Vice Presidents Richard Nixon and Hubert Humphrey, for example, were strengthened immeasurably by the support they received from delegates in party convention states that they had cultivated over the years.

Senator Eugene McCarthy's volunteers, however, charged repeatedly throughout the late spring and early summer of 1968, and especially after the assassination of Senator Robert F. Kennedy, that arch-rival Vice President Hubert H. Humphrey was using the Democratic state party organizations and old-guard professionals in the party convention states to deny McCarthy partisans a fair share of the state convention delegates. McCarthy's supporters argued that rank-and-file Democrats had no opportunity to say whether or not they wanted Humphrey to be their leader, since Humphrey had not entered any presidential primaries. The McCarthyites pointed out that the presidential primary elections in California, Oregon, Indiana, and elsewhere showed almost 80 per cent of the voters casting their ballots against the Humphrey stand-in candidates or against the Johnson Administration. Moreover, the McCarthy partisans argued that the Gallup and Harris public opinion polls indicated that McCarthy was running neck-and-neck with Vice President Humphrey in "trial heats" against former Vice President Richard M. Nixon. However, the McCarthyites ignored the

TABLE 2.5   **Gallop Poll, McCarthy-Humphrey "Showdown,"
            (Among Democrats)**

	1968 Late July	1968 Mid-August	1968 Late August
Humphrey	53%	46%	56%
McCarthy	38%	42%	38%
No Opinion	9%	12%	
Not Sure			6%
	100%	100%	100%

Source: Gallup and Harris polls, cited by Richard M. Scammon and Ben J. Wallenberg, The Real
Majority (1970), p. 148.

fact that Humphrey consistently out-polled McCarthy in those
Gallup polls which asked rank-and-file Democrats to list their
preferred candidate for President (see Table 2.5).

Scammon and Wattenberg, in reply to the argument that the
delegates are not responsive to the "party" will, have noted

. . . that in the convention of 1968, as in every Presidential
nominating convention of the past quarter of a century except
one [the GOP in 1964] the choice of the party's tens of millions
of adherents across the nation has also been the selection of
the national nominating convention.[17]

More will be said about "representativeness" of national conventions in Chapter Six.

Presidential Primaries

The formal process of selecting delegates to the national nominating conventions remained basically unchanged in the nineteenth century. But by the beginning of the twentieth century
leaders of the Progressive movement who had been waging an
unrelenting battle against the corrupt rule of political rings suc-

ceeded in passing direct primary legislation to take control of nominations for state and local office for the vested interests and put it into the hands of the voters. At the same time the Progressives in a number of states also sought to sidetrack boss control of delegate selection to the national conventions by giving this responsibility to the voters presidential primary elections. The Progressives reasoned that if the direct primary could be used to take power away from the powerful interests to choose nominees for state and local office, why couldn't the system be applied to presidential nominations as well?

From 1904 to America's entry in World War I, the Progressive forces in twenty-six states passed presidential primary laws to give the people a voice in the selection of their party nominees. The Progressives used two approaches—or a combination of two—to bring presidential nominations under popular control. In some states the reformers passed laws which provided for the direct election of delegates to national conventions (and, in some cases, for instruction of the delegates as to the popular preference for President). In the other states the reformers adopted only the presidential preference primary, which enabled the party electorate to express its choice for President. The term "presidential primary" is applied to all of these laws.[18]

Some of the reformers believed that the national party convention eventually should merely ratify the choice for President as

1972 PRESIDENTIAL PRIMARIES

State	Primary Date	State	Primary Date
New Hampshire	March 7	North Carolina	May 6
Florida	March 14	Nebraska	May 9
Illinois	March 21	West Virginia	May 9
Wisconsin	April 4	Maryland	May 16
Massachusetts	April 25	Oregon	May 23
Pennsylvania	April 25	Rhode Island	May 23
District		California	June 6
of Columbia	May 2	New Jersey	June 6
Indiana	May 2	New Mexico	June 6
Alabama	May 2	South Dakota	June 6
Ohio	May 2	New York	June 20
Tennessee	May 4	Arkansas	June 27

© 1972 by The New York Times Company. Reprinted by permission.

determined in the state presidential primaries. Among the leading planks of Theodore Roosevelt's Progressive party of 1912 was a recommendation for a nationwide presidential primary. President Woodrow Wilson, in his first message to Congress in 1913, called for a national presidential primary law. But these proposals received a cool reception in Congress—some critics said that an amendment to the U.S. Constitution would be needed to establish a nationwide primary. In any event, the presidential primary movement fell into decline after World War I—eight states abandoned their laws by 1935—as most presidential candidates dismissed these primaries as unimportant in their nomination plans.

After World War II, however, a resurgence of interest in the presidential primary occurred as several presidential candidates—Harold Stassen, a former governor of Minnesota, Senator Estes Kefauver of Tennessee, General Dwight D. Eisenhower, and Senator John F. Kennedy—recognized that a popular mandate won in contested presidential primaries might serve as a springboard to the White House.[19] More will be said later about the powerful impact of presidential primary victories upon state party leaders and the uncommitted convention delegates in our general assessment of the national convention system.

Recently, there has been a marked revival of interest of presidential primary legislation in the states as we approach the 1972 election. Six states—Michigan, New Mexico, Rhode Island, North Carolina, Tennessee, and Maryland—adopted presidential primary laws during 1969–72. Thus, as the 1972 presidential nominating race gets under way, at least twenty-three states and the District of Columbia will be using some form of the primary to elect convention delegates or to give the voters an opportunity to register their personal preference for President. In a few states the voters will have a combination of both options. Approximately two-thirds of the delegates to the 1972 national conventions will be elected from states using presidential primaries.

The reader should be aware that presidential candidates are not required to enter and campaign for delegates in all twenty primaries—in fact, this is one criticism made of the existing presidential primary system. Candidates can pick and choose the primaries they wish to enter. But nine states use what has been called a compulsory or "force primary" whereby all leading candidates are automatically included on the primary ballot by the secretary of state or an electoral commission—unless the candidate signs an affadavit disavowing his candidacy. The net effect of these compulsory primaries is to assure the voters of these states that they will have a good presidential foot race in at least one party every four years. Meanwhile, the national audience, in turn, and especially the national convention delegates in the non-primary states are all given a full view and opportunity to evaluate the performances of the various contenders. As the primary campaign unfolds and the various challengers meet head-on (some fall by the wayside), nationwide onlookers have ringside seats via television to judge which of the contestants has the superior qualifications, temperament, stamina, and understanding of the issues to be formally nominated by their party as candidates for President of the United States.

Delegate Selection by Committee

Of the 2,622 delegates attending the Democratic National Convention in 1968, the McGovern Commission discovered that 327 delegates (12.9 per cent) were selected by state party committees. This number, larger than expected, reflects the continuing influence of party leadership in delegation selection process. As noted earlier, four state Democratic parties—Arizona, Arkansas, Maryland, and Rhode Island—plus one territory, Puerto Rico, picked their entire national convention delegations by party committees in 1968. In four other states—New York, Oklahoma, Pennsylvania, and Washington—a portion of the delegation was chosen by party committees. These figures ranged from one-third in New York to one-half those in Oklahoma. Republican delegate selection procedures in the states mentioned above, while varying slightly, did not differ significantly.

The McGovern Commission report observed that "Committee systems offer only indirect participation in the selection process." Even more critical, the McGovern report continued: "states which permit the selection of delegates by party committees often leave other decisions which fundamentally affect the selection of delegates to the decision of the party committee itself."[20]

Now that methods of delegate selection have been spelled out, let's take a brief cross-section view of the types of persons who serve as delegates.

Who Are the Delegates?

According to several surveys, delegates in both parties are from the upper-middle and higher-income brackets.[21] In this respect they are not a representative cross-section of rank-and-file voters. In view of the fact that delegates in virtually all states (except North Dakota) are expected to pay all of their own convention expenses—$500 to $1,000, depending upon distance from convention, etc.—this prevalence of affluent delegates should come as no surprise, though it means that many able, potential delegates must forego attendance because it is too expensive.

EDUCATION, OCCUPATION, AND GROUP AFFILIATION

Approximately four-fifths of the delegates have attended college, and more than one-third have completed college and also some graduate work. Lawyers constitute about forty per cent of the convention delegations. According to available data, approximately one-quarter of all delegates to recent conventions have been businessmen, and one-eighth have been professional people (physicians, educators, engineers, etc.). Homemakers have constituted about five per cent of the delegates. Although some critics may regard the terms *Democratic party* and *organized labor* as almost indistinguishable, studies in 1948, 1952, and 1964 showed that only about ten per cent of the Democratic delegates were union members. In 1948, only one delegate in fifteen called himself a farmer or rancher, although sixteen per cent of the delegates belonged to the Farm Bureau, according to a study by Dan Tuttle.[22]

AGE-SEX-RACE   Over the years, serving as delegates to national conventions has been mostly a middle-age, white male avocation. Young people, women, and blacks have been distinctly in the minority as data on the 1968 Democratic convention delegates listed in Table 2.6 (pp. 30–31) indicate.

AGE   The bulk of the delegates at both Democratic and GOP conventions have been men in their forties and fifties. At the 1968 Democratic National Convention 16 delegations had no voting members under the age of 30, another 13 delegations had only one delegate under 30 years old. The record of the Republicans was even worse. At the 1968 GOP convention in Miami Beach only 1 per cent of the GOP delegates were under the age of 30 years. In 42 states there were no voting delegates under 30, and in an additional 8 delegations, there was only one member under 30. Approximately 83 per cent of the GOP delegates were 40 years of age or older.[23] But in light of the widespread demands for reform, especially in the Democratic party, the average age level of delegates can be expected to drop in the years ahead. Passage of the 26th Amendment should bring many more young people to the conventions as both parties assiduously court the young voters. Indeed, competition alone for their votes will force both parties to open their doors to more young people.

SEX   Although women now comprise a majority of the voting age population in the United States, they have often found delegate positions at national conventions to be beyond their reach. In the 1968 Democratic convention, for example, women comprised only 13 per cent of the voting delegates. As the McGovern Commission report noted, "In no state were women represented commensurate to their presence in the population; in ten delegations there were insufficient women to fulfill positions traditionally assigned to them on the four permanent committees of the convention."[24]

In Ohio, only 6 of 116 Democratic delegates were women, and in the Illinois delegation, dominated by Mayor Richard Daley of Chicago, only 8 of 118 delegates were women. Representative

TABLE 2.6   **Representation of Young People, Women, and Blacks at the 1968 Democratic National Convention by States (as percent of each delegation)**

	Total Number of Delegates	Percent Under 30	Percent Women	Percent Blacks
Alabama	50	8	14	4
Alaska	22	5	5	0
Arizona	34	0	21	3
Arkansas	54	2	22	2
California	174	5	14	5
Colorado	42	0	14	8
Connecticut	44	0	16	7
Delaware	22	0	9	5
Florida	63	5	44	7
Georgia	88	9	19	26
Hawaii	26	4	8	0
Idaho	26	0	15	0
Illinois	118	1	9	6
Indiana	68	0	6	8
Iowa	52	4	17	2
Kansas	42	0	24	3
Kentucky	62	3	20	8
Louisiana	52	4	10	18
Maine	30	3	13	0
Maryland	49	0	8	6
Massachusetts	83	1	12	3
Michigan	102	1	19	20
Minnesota	62	3	18	5
Mississippi	45	7	7	50
Missouri	78	1	15	4
Montana	32	3	25	0
Nebraska	30	20	23	0
Nevada	30	10	17	7
New Hampshire	26	8	12	0
New Jersey	82	0	12	9
New Mexico	34	6	12	0
New York	236	1	9	6
No. Carolina	74	1	10	6
No. Dakota	25	4	28	0
Ohio	125	0	6	3
Oklahoma	58	5	21	9
Oregon	35	9	23	0
Pennsylvania	164	5	11	5
Rhode Island	34	0	12	3
So. Carolina	42	0	5	13
So. Dakota	26	4	23	0

	Total Number of Delegates	Percent Under 30	Percent Women	Percent Blacks
Tennessee	66	0	9	11
Texas	121	1	12	4
Utah	26	0	23	0
Vermont	22	5	18	0
Virginia	65	2	11	6
Washington	54	7	14	0
W. Virginia	38	11	5	2
Wisconsin	62	3	19	0
Wyoming	28	0	18	0
District of Columbia	23	9	35	67
Canal Zone	8	0	50	(a)
Guam	8	0	13	(a)
Puerto Rico	14	0	21	(a)
Virgin Islands	8	0	13	(a)
TOTAL	3,084	4	13	

1. The ages of all delegates were not available to the Commission; therefore, the percentage of young people indicated may be taken to indicate a minimum proportion of each state's delegation.
2. Distinguish total number of delegates and total number of delegate votes. In 1968, 3,084 delegates cast 2,622 votes.

(a) Information not available.

Source: Mandate for Reform A Report of the Commission on Party Structure and Delegate Selection to the Democratic National Committee (McGovern Commission Report). Washington D.C. Democratic National Committee, April 1970, pp. 27–28.

Edith Green of Oregon served as the only woman chairman of the fifty-five state and territorial delegations. Figures from recent GOP conventions showed that the percentage of women at Republican conventions has been slightly higher than at Democratic conclaves.[25] In the 1968 GOP convention women comprised 17 per cent of the delegates. Two states (New Hampshire and West Virginia) and the Virgin Islands, however, had no women at all in their delegations. Eleven state delegations did not have

the four women required to fill the places assigned to them on
the four standing committees of the GOP conventions.

RACE   Though Negroes now constitute over 11 per cent of the
population, they have always been underrepresented in ratio to
population at both the Republican and Democratic national conventions. The GOP seems to be less concerned than the Democratic party about permitting Negro delegates to serve as delegates. At the 1968 Republican convention in Miami only 76
delegates (2.4 per cent) were black. Of these only 26 were actually
voting delegates (1.9 per cent of the total delegates) and 50 were
alternates. Only fourteen state GOP delegations contained black
members. In 1964 only 14 Negro delegates (1.07 per cent) attended the San Francisco GOP convention.

Approximately 5.5 per cent of the delegates to the 1968 Democratic convention were black, in contrast to only 2 per cent in
1964. Thirteen states and three territories still had no black delegates or alternates whatever and fifteen had no voting delegates.
Another eleven states had only one black member, and six more
had three or less.[26]

In the GOP most of the Negro delegates have come from the
Southern states since the Civil War. Most of the Democratic Negro delegates have been from the North, though this was less
true at the 1968 Democratic convention in Chicago, which
authorized integrated Southern delegations from Mississippi
and Georgia.

PUBLIC AND PARTY OFFICE   Ostrogorski's turn-of-the-cen-
tury observation about the large number of public and party
officials attending national conventions is still valid.[27] High-level
public officials constitute between twelve and eighteen percent
of the delegations. In 1956, thirty-four governors were members
of delegations; many of them were delegation chairmen. Nearly
two-thirds of the United States Senators were also members of
delegations in 1956. At the 1968 GOP convention 42 per cent of
the delegates had held public office.[28] Party officeholders, especially state, district, and county chairmen, are an important vot-

ing bloc in nearly all state delegations. In 1960, approximately 85 per cent of New York Democratic delegation consisted of persons either holding down government jobs or active in the party. More than half of the Empire State's sixty-three county chairmen attended the 1960 Democratic convention, mostly as delegates rather than as alternates.[29]

FREQUENCY OF CONVENTION ATTENDANCE   According to a 1956 survey on recent conventions, approximately 40 per cent of the delegates had attended previous conventions at least once. Approximately 30 per cent had attended two consecutive conventions; 10 to 12 per cent had attended three. Beyond this point, however, the percentage attending four or more conventions declined sharply.

Recently, William Baum and his fellow researchers have discovered that delegate turnover at GOP conventions has been relatively high—somewhat higher than expected. Between two-thirds and three-fourths of the GOP delegates did not return to the next convention. Only 31 per cent of all GOP delegates in 1968 had attended the 1964 conclave. Earlier, only 27.3 per cent of those Republicans (including alternates) who were at the 1960 GOP convention were at the 1964 San Francisco convention.[30] Within a span of three GOP conventions (1956 through 1964) eleven states had a complete turnover in their delegations; thirteen states had only one holdover delegate. In short, almost half the states had a complete turnover or were within one delegate of a complete turnover within an eight-year period.[31] For young political activists the opportunities for upward political mobility within the party hierarchy are patently evident.

DELEGATE ATTITUDES   Until an extensive study by Herbert McClosky on the opinions and attitudes of approximately 3,000 delegates attending the 1956 GOP and Democratic conventions, no solid data were available on delegate attitudes. McClosky found, in comparing the reaction of delegates with a 15,000-person nationwide Gallup Poll survey of the general population, that party leaders of the two major parties hold far more divergent views on issues than do rank-and-file members who differ only moderately.

McClosky's data also showed that convention delegates were more willing to draw sharp lines between liberal and conservative groups and to take firm stands on the issues. Among the party rank-and-file, political apathy was more prevalent than concern over issues. On the twenty-four major issues polled, GOP "followers" disagreed frequently with the Republican delegates, classified as "leaders."[32] According to McClosky, GOP delegates were far more conservative on issues than the rank-and-filers; indeed, these "grass-roots" members were closer to Democratic delegates on issues preference. While Democratic leaders and followers disagreed on some issues, this occurred with much less frequency. McClosky's data also revealed that Republicans were generally united on issues that arose from the party's association with business groups. Democratic delegates appeared to be in general agreement on issues relating to low-income groups.[33] These are the delegates, then, who select the presidential nominees.

The various activities sketched in this chapter are illustrative of one of the four standard convention functions: government of the party. Now, let's move on to the hurly-burly, crush, and confusion of a typical national convention.

CONVENTION COMMITTEE ACTIVITY

The mounting tempo of excitement that accompanies the national convention can be detected several days before the curtain rises at the quadrennial extravanganza. Already the headquarters of the various contenders are operating at a frantic pace. To add to the excitement and confusion, hundreds of television network staff personnel and newsmen descend upon the convention city to report on "the greatest show on earth." In 1964, the Associated Press reported that members of the news media outnumbered delegates and alternates to the Republican national convention in San Francisco by a 3-to-1 margin. There were 1,308 delegates and an equal number of alternates—2,616 in all; according to the Republican public relations staff, 7,000 representatives of the television and news media were on hand to report the events.[1]

By the time the fifty state delegations and territorial representatives begin flocking into the convention city the weekend before the opening sessions, the platform committee has already been hard at work for several days putting the final touches on the careful phraseology of the various planks.[2] The credentials committee will also be in session, striving to arrive at an amicable compromise on contested delegation controversies or merely checking out the delegates' documentation, if there are no challenges. Until 1972, all of these major convention committees in both parties provided equal representation to all fifty states in the Union—another recognition of the confederate nature of American parties. Thus, the Platform Committee in each party had two members, one man and one woman, from each state; the same arrangement was also followed on the other regular committee. But at the 1972 Democratic convention large states with a heavy Democratic vote will be given weighted representation.

The final pre-convention hours will be marked by various party festivities—receptions, cocktail parties, dinners, and

caucus meetings among the various delegations—as the tension
builds up and the curtain rises on the great political drama.

Order of Business

Despite the carnival-like atmosphere of the convention, the
usual order of business does not vary much from one convention
to the next. On the first day (usually a Monday) the delegates will
hear the various welcoming addresses, approve the installation
of temporary officers and appointment of committees (which
have been tentatively selected several months earlier by the national committee), and listen to the keynote address.

The chief item of business on the second day is devoted to the
committee reports. It is at this time that heated floor fights over
the seating of contested delegations may take place. Once these
disputes have been settled, the convention is ready to consider
the party platform.

The climax of the convention comes on the third day with the
nomination of the various presidential contenders. Nominating
speeches and balloting for the party's presidential candidate
may extend to an eight-hour session—and into the next day, if
necessary.

The fourth day of the convention is somewhat anti-climatic as
the delegates select the vice-presidential candidate—usually the
hand-picked choice of the presidential nominee. After the two
nominees for the national ticket make their formal acceptance
speeches, the curtain then rings down for another four years.
The delegates then turn homeward, emotionally exhausted from
nearly a week of sleepless nights and endless speeches, but usually confident that their party is destined for victory in November. Not for another four years will the supreme governing body
of the national party convene again for another ritualistic series
of tribal rites that presage the nomination of another presidential candidate—or the renomination of an incumbent. Let's take
a few moments to review the step-by-step operation of a typical
national convention.

Before the delegates sit back to hear the keynote speaker

deliver an old-fashioned political speech praising his own party to the rafters while thoroughly blistering the opposition party, the temporary chairman is usually installed in routine fashion. If there is a floor fight over the temporary chairmanship (which is rare), one can usually detect signs of a badly-divided party. The deep cleavages within the Republican party in 1912 came to the surface during this opening session, as the Taft and Roosevelt factions squared off to battle over the temporary chairman (won by the Taft forces). Usually, however, agreement on the temporary chairman and keynote speaker has already been ironed out at earlier planning sessions of the national committee.

Selection of Permanent Officers and Action of Committee Reports

On the second day of the convention the party officers and committee chairmen begin to roll up their sleeves for the serious business ahead. First, on the agenda is the report of the Committee on Permanent Organization with its recommendation for the permanent chairman of the convention and other regular officers. Ordinarily, the delegates endorse these selections *pro forma.* Indeed, the name of the scheduled permanent chairman has already been publicized for several months, since his name has been proposed at an earlier meeting of the party's national committee. The last big fight over the permanent chairmanship occurred in 1932, between the forces of Governor Franklin Delano Roosevelt and the 1928 Democratic presidential nominee, Alfred E. Smith. The selection of Roosevelt's choice—Senator Thomas Walsh of Montana—was the tip-off that FDR held the inside track for the nomination, which he won on the fourth ballot.[3]

The strategic importance of the permanent chairman's power of recognition and his rulings on motions for a recess or adjournment on the day's proceedings can sometimes be decisive. In 1940, for example, Senator John Bricker of Ohio, a key backer of his fellow Ohioan—the late Senator Robert A. Taft—moved for a recess before the crucial sixth ballot. This recess might have enabled the Taft and Dewey forces to make a deal and thereby halt the surging Willkie drive. Chairman Joseph Martin, who was sympathatic to the Willkie cause, refused the request; Willkie won the nomination on the sixth ballot.[4] The advent of televised convention proceedings has probably lessened the possibility of cavalier or unfair rulings from the chair (for fear of alienating many independent voters watching), but the role of the permanent chairman should not be underestimated.

As soon as the permanent chairman has been installed, the other three major committees—Rules, Credentials, and Platform —offer their reports. It is at this juncture sometimes that the fireworks start.

Rules

At the 1968 Democratic National Convention a heated controversy developed over the so-called "unit rule," requiring all members of a state delegation instructed under this rule to vote according to the wishes of the delegation majority. Earlier, the McCarthyites had pushed supporters of Vice President Humphrey, the front-running contender, to join forces to put an end to the unit rule. This strategy was aimed at several Southern delegations still adhering to the unit rule. Unhappily for Humphrey, most of these Southerners were Humphrey backers. After a short, heated debate the unit rule was abolished on a voice vote.[5] Not only was the unit rule declared illegal at the 1968 and all future national conventions, but the committee report also stated that the unit rule should not be used in any state or local party proceedings either. An attempt by the Humphreyites to mollify the huge 104-member Texas delegation (which used the unit rule) by delaying application of the unit rule until the 1972 national convention was voted down with a resounding "no."[6]

In 1952 the Republicans "averted" a head-on collision between the Eisenhower-Taft forces over the permanent rules only because this confrontation had already occurred earlier on the normally routine motion to adopt the temporary rules. Twenty years earlier, Governor Franklin D. Roosevelt's partisans avoided a potentially disastrous clash over the historic "two-thirds" rule by dropping their earlier plans to move its repeal.[7]

Credentials

Major convention battles have often revolved around the credentials of contesting rival delegations from one-party states. Until recently, southern Republican organizations usually consisted of self-appointed party officials who presided over thinly-populated GOP constituencies and then selected themselves as delegates to the national conventions. Whenever the chances of a Republican presidential victory were bright, the impending possibility of federal patronage in the area often attracted a second, competing GOP group—also self-appointed—into the delegate contests. Since each of the rival factions usually identified with a major presidential contender or the conservative and liberal factions within the national party, the odds were high that the two factional groups would collide before GOP Credentials Committee. It is almost a rule-of-thumb that the convention's decision on the seating of these competing delegations has portended which major candidate would win the nomination. President William Howard Taft's victory in the 1912 GOP credentials fight and Eisenhower's triumph over the Robert A. Taft partisans in the 1952 credentials controversy are the best-known cases.

In recent years, the Democratic conventions have been the scene of bitter controversy over the same general question—the credentials of competing southern delegations. Unlike the GOP, most Democratic credentials fights have been offshoots of the civil rights movement, not the case of two rotten borough delegations quarreling over patronage plums.

At the 1964 Atlantic City convention, a credentials fight emerged over the question of whether the regular Mississippi Democratic party could systematically discriminate against Negroes in the selection of delegates. When the dust had cleared, the integrated Free Democratic Party of Mississippi had won only token representation. But the 1964 Democratic National

Convention adopted a rule prohibiting such discriminatory practices against blacks in the future.[8] At the 1968 Chicago convention this issue added fuel to an already volatile battle between the forces of the Vice President Humphrey and Senator Eugene McCarthy. Challenges by integrated delegations against the segregationist old-guard Democratic delegations in Mississippi, Georgia, Texas, and Alabama were reviewed, first by the credentials committee and then by the full convention. To the chagrin of many veteran Southern Democrats, the convention refused to seat the "regular," all-white Mississippi Democratic delegation, replacing it with an integrated, moderate group. In a close decision on the Georgia contest the convention voted to seat both the conservative, "regular" Georgia delegation and the integrated, McCarthy-oriented delegation led by Julian Bond, a young Georgia Negro legislator—each group receiving half of the allotted votes for Georgia.[9] The predominantly-segregationist Texas and Alabama delegations, after the fight of their lives, won their seats by narrow margins. It seems safe to predict, however, that we have not seen the last of the contested delegation fights, at least under the present convention rules. They are almost as much a part of the convention activity as the keynote speaker or platform-making.

Party Platform

Toward the end of the second day or early in the third, the chairman of the Committee on Resolutions and Platform is asked to make his report. The platform presentation represents the culmination of several weeks labor by the committee members and their staff assistants. And it's important to remember that "platform-drafting, like the nominating process, is highly political."[10]

The platforms of both parties usually are the results of candidate pressure and lobbying action by interest groups as well as the deliberations of platform committees. Interest groups at national conventions have two major goals: the nomination of a friendly presidential candidate and the inclusion of favorable planks in the platform. To achieve their goals, the interest groups may seek representation in state delegations (the Michigan Democratic party delegation, for example, will usually contain twenty or twenty-five trade unionists—at least one-quarter of the delegation). Also, they may lobby before the convention platform committee. Interest groups will usually receive a sympathetic hearing from the platform committee, for the political party and the presidential candidate need the support of organized groups as much as these groups need the party's backing.[11] The mass membership organizations, for example, the United Auto Workers or the Farm Bureau, can encourage their members to turn out in force on election day. Organizations can provide parties with the sinews of war in the form of money or trained workers to conduct registration drives and other campaign activities.

The platform may be read in its entirety or only key sections (television audiences do not relish listening to entire platforms). Then the chairman moves its adoption. Sometimes it will be approved in routine fashion, particularly if a majority of the convention delegates have just about agreed informally on their nominee. Television viewers of the 1968 GOP national convention, for example, heard the mellifluous tones of the Platform Chairman, the late Senator Everett McKinley Dirksen, as he conducted the platform proceedings. For a brief moment viewers saw Governor George Romney of Michigan rise to explain briefly why he was not going to offer a platform amendment aimed at the monopolistic practices of unions. With this procedural matter handled, the convention wasted no time in approving the platform by a voice vote.[12] Then, the flamboyant Dirksen tossed a batch of papers (whether they were copies of the platform is unknown) to the audience, as if he were feeding pigeons on the Capitol steps.

The low esteem that most American voters hold for platform-making is generally exceeded only by their ignorance of the contents of these party documents. Nor do the party platforms generate much enthusiasm among the party faithful. This disinterest mirrors the general view that party platforms have little rela-

tionship to subsequent governmental policy-making. Gerald
Pomper has summarized the charges as follows:

1. Platform statements are essentially unimportant, ambiguous, and often contradictory. . . .
2. No differences exist between the platforms of the major
   parties. They are therefore of no value to the voter in making his choice of party.
3. The party principles are not binding on party candidates.
   The principle object of the platform is, in the present day,
   as formerly, to catch votes by trading on the credulity of the
   electors. . . .[13]

On the surface these criticisms seem valid. But party platforms
are not just so much rhetoric, as the critics claim. Polsby and
Wildavsky have noted, "Party platforms written by the presidential parties should be understood not as ends in themselves but
as a means to obtaining and holding public office.[14] The careful
reader of the party platforms will be able to discern, over a
period of time, long-term policy differences that accurately reflect significant distinctions between Democrats and Republicans on such issues as medicare, federal-aid-to-education, civil
rights, housing, and the economy. Though not a typical example,
the distinctions between Republican and Democratic platforms
were plainly evident in 1964 when the GOP platform, drafted by
Goldwater partisans, echoed the Arizonian's arch-conservative
views. In contrast, the Democratic platform forecast President
Lyndon B. Johnson's broad-gauged "Great Society" legislative
program enacted in 1965—largely forgotten after President
Johnson pushed the country ever more deeply into the Vietnamese conflict.

Still, several presidential candidates elected to the White
House have refused to be bound by platform provisions when it
seemed expedient or unwise. Arch-critics of President Franklin
D. Roosevelt, for example, never tired of reminding him that the
1932 Democratic platform pledged to reduce government expenditures during the bottom of the Great Depression; yet within six
months after taking office, FDR launched the country on a vast

"pump-priming" program to stimulate the sagging economy—at the cost of a huge deficit during his first term. Another more recent illustration will be found in the 1964 Democratic platform. This document pledged to limit American involvement in Vietnam, but within a year President Johnson had sent more than 250,000 American troops to block the attempted Viet Cong-North Vietnamese takeover of South Vietnam.

If platforms can be ignored, the question might be legitimately asked, why do parties go to such great length to quibble over specific provisions? Even more basic, why have platforms at all? Why not have the two rival presidential candidates delineate their own position on the issues during the course of the campaign?

The answer to these questions will be found within the internal dynamics of American parties.[15] Rarely, if ever, are American parties united on all major policy issues. Though factionalism is endemic to the American party system, it undoubtedly produces also much of the vitality found in our parties. From one election to the next the liberal and conservative wings within each party will be vying for control. Some veteran party-watchers are convinced that there is as much rivalry within parties as between the major parties. On the national level this factionalism is most likely to come to the surface at the quadrennial conventions. Factionalism between rival wings of the party, of course, can also be found on Capitol Hill as the liberal and conservative leaders within each party seek to control legislative activity. But the high stakes of the Presidency and its domination of the national government make this office the focal point of a major tug-of-war between competing factions. At the national conventions, this rivalry is most likely to come to the surface during the consideration of the platform. That platform-making can throw a spotlight on intra-party power struggles has occurred frequently in modern party history, indeed, twice during the past decade. The 1964 GOP and the 1968 Democratic party platform fights are the most recent cases.

At the 1964 Republican Convention, Senator Barry Goldwater supporters, who dominated the platform committee, drafted an

arch-conservative platform that right-wing Republicans had
been demanding for more than a generation. Belatedly, the liberal and moderate Republicans realized at the eleventh hour
that their only hope for blocking Goldwater's nomination depended upon a frontal-assault on his right-wing "extremism"
—as evidenced in the various platform planks hammered out by
the pro-Goldwater majority.

The anti-Goldwaterites decided to make their stand on key
issues of civil rights, extremist political groups, and civilian control of the military. When the platform was presented to the
convention for adoption, leading spokesmen from the moderate
wing moved several amendments from the floor calling for ex-
plicit approval of the Civil Rights Act of 1964 (which Goldwater
had voted against) and outright condemnation of the Ku Klux
Klan and the John Birch Society (whose support Goldwater
refused to disavow). The highlight of the anti-Goldwater drive
took place when his chief rival, Governor Nelson Rockefeller,
mounted the rostrum to argue on behalf of one of the proposed
amendments. He was met with a barrage of catcalls, jeers, and
obscenities that drowned out many of his remarks. For several
minutes Rockefeller could not be heard. Convention Chairman
Thruston Morton finally restored sufficient order to enable Rockefeller to complete his statement. All of the amendments were
flatly rejected by the pro-Goldwater majority, which then endorsed the full platform. The next day the convention approved
Goldwater as the nominee by a resounding majority.[16] But the
platform fight, which reflected the deep rift within the GOP,
foretold of an impending disaster—the GOP went down to defeat
in November, losing by nearly 16 million votes.

Platform-making at the 1968 Democratic Convention was not
merely a parliamentary exercise either, for it revealed a deep
schism within the Democratic party over the issue of the Vietnamese war. Indeed, it was on this single issue that the leading
anti-war challenger Senator Eugene McCarthy waged his fight
for the Democratic nomination. By sponsoring a floor fight over
the minority proposal on Vietnam which called for an "uncondi-
tional end" to all bombing on North Vietnam, McCarthy hoped

to split the party ranks and attract enough support to capture the
nomination from the front-runner—Vice President Humphrey.
In an attempt to head off the McCarthy attack, the Humphrey
forces initially tried to draft a Vietnamese plank that would sat-
isfy some of the "dove" delegates and play down the Vietnam
issue. But the pro-Humphrey majority plank, drafted behind-
the-scenes with some stern coaching from President Johnson,
offered a conditional cessation of the bombing and proposed to
reduce military involvement "as the South Vietnamese forces
are able to take over their large responsibilities." The minority
proposal on this second point pledged an immediate de-escalation, making possible "an early withdrawal of a significant number of our troops." Senator McCarthy, in attacking the pro-
Administration Vietnam plank, declared that the choice "was
between those who want more of the same and those who think
it is necessary to change our course in Vietnam."[17]

Thus, the battle lines between the Humphrey and McCarthy
partisans were clearly drawn for the show down platform fight
over Vietnam. The Johnson Administration forces running the
convention originally sought to schedule the platform proceedings during the late evening hours of the second day, after most
TV-viewers in the East had gone to bed. But as the session
dragged on past midnight, delayed by the seating contests, the
anti-Administration dissidents sought to postpone the platform
discussion until the next afternoon with shouts of "Let's go home!
let's go home!" Amidst the pandemonium, Convention Chairman
Carl Albert, taking a cue from Mayor Daley of Chicago, adjourned the session until the next afternoon. To the surprise of
some observers, the two-hour platform debate on Vietnam offered an unusually open and high-level exchange of views by
prominent party spokesmen. Senator Edmund Muskie of Maine,
speaking for the majority and subsequently nominated Vice-
President, expressed the view that the broad areas of agreement
existed between the two opposing camps. Ted Sorenson, the
former aide to President John F. Kennedy, made the most elo-
quent plea for the minority: "If you cannot give our young people
and the amateurs and the idealists the candidate of their choice,

at least give them this plank to preserve their enthusiasm for the Democratic Party."[18]

When the debate time-limit expired on the Vietnam plank, the roll-call showed the majority report prevailing 1,567 3/4 to 1,041 1/4 votes. The outcome of the platform debate signaled the collapse of the McCarthy candidacy (and a short-lived boomlet for Senator Ted Kennedy), thereby removing all doubt that Humphrey would be the Democratic standard-bearer. Some Democratic leaders had hoped that the public airing of the Vietnam issue in the platform debate would be a catharsis to bring the party together for the fall campaign. More pessimistic party leaders concluded that the rupture would cost the Democrats the Presidency in 1968. Vice President Humphrey lost the Presidential race, as had been freely predicted by the party "doves"—though by the narrow popular margin of 517,777 votes.

Significantly, the 1968 convention's minority report position on the unilateral withdrawal of troops from Vietnam became within a year the prevailing position on Vietnam for a near majority of Democrats on Capitol Hill and by mid-1970 a majority rank-and-file party members throughout the country. The impact of the "great convention debate" over Vietnam lived long after the delegates returned to their homes, and the country under a new Republican administration began an American de-escalation of the war in Southeast Asia. Generally, though, the party platform is a means of achieving a majority coalition of factions and this helps accord recognition to the variegated power groups within a party.[19] During the convention and afterwards, these diverse groups can point to various planks in the party platform that specifically recognize their individual status.

Platform-making helps strengthen the cohesiveness of the party by enabling minority factions that fail to nominate their Presidential candidate to win some measure of success. In other words, they do not leave the convention empty-handed. As Polsby and Wildavsky have observed: "The platform tests and communicates the ability of the many party factions to agree on something, even if on some crucial points major differences have to be papered over."[20]

Platform-making for the party out of power is a negotiation process through which the various factions may receive their rewards or pay-offs before the presidential nominations start. If the platform were to be approved after the Presidential nominee had been selected, it would generate much less interest and would lose much of its viability as a consensus-building instrument. Furthermore, the winning nominee would be held fully accountable for its contents, thereby cutting down his campaign discretion and governing latitude.

To protect an incumbent President seeking a second term from having to fulfill impossible platform promises, the White House will invariably have several presidential assistants attached to the committee. In fact, the White House staffers usually draft all of the key provisions in the various planks. It's an open secret that President Johnson personally okayed the entire 1964 Democratic Party platform before it was submitted to the delegates for ratification. And at the 1968 Chicago convention, Johnson, though not a candidate for reelection, had a trusted adviser overseeing the platform drafts on the Vietnam issue. The situation has been no different at GOP conventions. At the 1968 Republican national convention in Miami Beach, the platform committee was under the full control of front-runner Richard Nixon's lieutenants. In 1964 the Rockefeller supporters at the San Francisco convention soon discovered, if they did not already know, that the Goldwater forces had taken over the platform-writing duties, along with their tight-reined control of the nomination proceedings. And it's a foregone conclusion that several of President Nixon's special assistants will personally oversee the drafting of the 1972 GOP platform when he presumably will seek a second term.

Effect of Party Platforms

While platforms may indicate much about future governmental action, they of course cannot provide a full blue-print for future action. In the first place, conditions may change. Programs outlined in the platform may become outdated. New prob- *

lems and contingencies may arise which could not be anticipated during the campaign. At best, the platform can only suggest the party's general approach to major problems. Furthermore, the platform cannot dictate future action because American parties are not centralized or disciplined organizations capable of implementing policy decisions by enforcing its positions on all members and legislators of the party. American parties are confederations of local and state organizations that lack sanctions to enforce a specific position upon the party.

The separation of powers, which often inhibits close legislative-executive cooperation, also affects the electoral process. The President, if elected, has no assurance that he can impose the platform pledges on his party in Congress. In the past twenty years (1952–1972) party control of the Presidency and Congress has been divided half of this period. But even if a President and a majority of Congress are from the same party, the congressional majority may repudiate the party pledges. This raises the basic question: can parties consistently fulfill their campaign pledges? The Democratic platform experiences in 1948 and the GOP's 1952 record are illustrative: The Truman Democratic Administration fulfilled pledges to: (1) establish a United Nations headquarters in the United States; (2) sign a peace treaty with Japan; (3) extend the Marshall Plan; (4) bring Israel into the United Nations; (5) provide federal aid to housing; (6) increase social security benefits; (7) raise the minimum wage; (8) provide fixed farm supports; (9) repeal marginal taxes; (10) admit displaced persons to the country; (11) extend the reciprocal trade acts. While this track record was high, unredeemed Democratic pledges included: federal aid to education, repeal of the Taft-Hartley labor union legislation; and supportive of civil rights.[21]

The first Eisenhower Administration had a similar platform record. The GOP met its pledges on the following: (1) support of European integration; (2) conclusion of the Korean war; (3) publication of Yalta documents; (4) reduction of the civil service; (5) elimination of federal price and wage controls; (6) reduction of corporate taxation; (7) ceding of jurisdiction over offshore oil deposits to the states; (8) restrictions on the Tennessee Valley

Authority; (9) an increase in the air force budget; (10) opposition to federal educational aid; (11) enactment of a Korean G. I. Bill of Rights. The GOP did not fulfill its pledges to seek full farm parity prices, pass civil rights bills; or amend the Taft-Hartley Act. By and large, the data show a remarkably good performance by both parties in fulfilling campaign pledges.[22]

As for the charge that platforms are ambiguous, a reading of several party platforms will show that the party document is vague and imprecise when the party tries to resolve or reconcile basic conflicts between competing forces within the party. As Pomper has noted, "When the party seeks to appeal to a wide range of interests, vagueness results. When the party feels that its electoral chances will be improved by an uncompromising appeal to one group, platforms will become clearer."[23] Pomper reminds us also that "the platform cannot reveal exactly *what* future positions of the party or the government will be. It can indicate who will be in control of the party and, if the party wins the elections, of the government."[24] For the individual voter and the interest groups concerned with the outcome of the election, knowledge of those political leaders responsible for drafting the platform is usually a tip-off on the future direction of policy changes. In David Truman's view, "The significance of preparing a platform lies primarily in the evidence that the negotiations provide concerning what groups will have access to the developing national party organization. . . . Interest group leaders are aware that the real settlement of the issues they are concerned with, even within the party, will take place later; in the platform they seek tentative assurance of a voice in that settlement."[25]

A party platform cannot be quietly slipped under the rug whenever electoral circumstances change. Indeed, Gerald Pomper has reminded us that for a party to ignore consistently its pledges "confuses the voters and also results in distrust of the party, to its ultimate detriment."[26] Briefly, then, the platform is a campaign document. And it belongs to the party, not the presidential candidate. As a party manifesto, it is a reasonably predictable indication of the party's intentions.[27] In Pomper's words,

"Platforms indeed are to run on, not to stand on—but they also can reflect and affect the pace, direction, winner and meaning of the race."[28]

Once the party platform has been approved, the delegates are ready to settle down to the main item of convention business: nominating and selecting the party's presidential candidate— the subject of our next chapter.

PRESIDENTIAL CONTENDERS AND THE MOMENT OF DECISION

As the contenders stand poised for the final stretch drive, it seems appropriate to ask two pertinent questions: Who are the presidential contenders? How did they become contenders for the highest office in the land?

Sidney Hyman, in his thoughtful study of the Presidency almost two decades ago, pointed out that of the 60,000,000 voters in the United States at the time not more than a hundred men could be considered serious candidates for President. Nor indeed is every political leader who becomes a governor or United States Senator regarded as presidential timber.[1] To differentiate between the public figures who are potentially serious presidential candidates and those who are not, professional politicians have developed the concept of "availability."

Presidential "Availability"

By "availability" we do not mean a person who merely aspires to high office, since many small-bore politicians have their sights set high. Availability means that one is capable of being elected President of the United States. A number of factors contribute to a candidate's availability, but the chief factor is evidence that the candidate has enough gilt-edge credentials to convince the party leaders and national convention delegates that he, the candidate, has enough vote-getting ability to reach the White House.

Availability criteria can be classified under the following general headings: political background, personal life and characteristics, geography, religion, a combined category of age-sex-race, and high "visibility" (easily identified). However, in "the making

51

of a President," no serious aspirant for the Presidency has ever scored 100 per cent in all categories. If a candidate holds a high public office and a record of accomplishment, a favorable "image" on television, and adequate financial backing to mount a hard-hitting pre-convention campaign, he can be considered to be "available." Beyond that, it is impossible to tell where political lightning may strike. Sometimes the fate of a candidate may rest upon factors unforeseen or uncontrollable. And no systematic analysis has been found that entirely rules out luck or the "breaks of the game." But Southern candidates, no matter how well qualified they may be, have been almost totally ignored by both major parties (except for Lyndon B. Johnson who originally filled out the unexpired term of President Kennedy in 1963) for two major reasons: First, the Republicans, as a result of their Reconstruction policies that alienated the South after the Civil War, wrote off—at least until the 1960's—the South as a lost cause. Secondly, the Democrats felt that they could carry the Solid South, irrespective of their candidate; hence, they preferred to pick candidates from the large, pivotal states of the North. With the surprising emergence of a two-party system in many parts of the South, it remains to be seen whether or not the boycott of Southern candidates will persist.

Availability, according to Gerald Pomper, has been replaced by new criteria, which might be termed "prominence."[2] More than a decade ago William Carleton also argued that in order to win the Presidency the candidate first needed to be a national "name" or "celebrity."[3] While Carleton may have overstated his case, the experience of recent conventions indicates that to become a serious contender a prospective nominee must be readily identifiable by the mass public. Indeed, the Gallup polling organization recently announced that in "trial heat" polls of various presidential contenders, a candidate needed to be recognized by 80 per cent of the electorate in order to give the candidate a fair chance in the poll.[4] In this fast-moving era a presidential candidate can utilize presidential primary contests, the public opinion polls, and the mass media to pyramid himself into front-runner contention and thereby "force himself on the attention of the convention."[5]

The present author, in another study, has argued that well-known "national" candidates in the out-of-power party have used contested presidential primary victories to knock out rival intra-party contenders and thereby lay claim to the nomination.[6] General Dwight Eisenhower, John F. Kennedy, and Richard M. Nixon (in 1968) all followed this route to win the nomination and subsequently the Presidency. All three of these winning nominees, of course, were highly "visible" candidates when they sought the nomination, with General Eisenhower, a victorious war hero, the best known of the three. Eisenhower, Nixon, and Kennedy did not meet all of the traditional availability criteria, that is, Eisenhower had not held public office; Kennedy was not a Protestant; and Nixon was a one-time presidential candidate "loser." But this inability to meet all the standard availability tests did not halt their drives for the Presidency.

"Availability," according to Pomper, has "applied most completely when conventions were controlled by state party organizations."[7] But state party organizations can no longer dominate the presidential nominating process in face of the challenges of mass democracy as reflected in the primaries, polls, and media. Indeed, "As the capacity to deal with the ultimate questions of peace and war become the principal test of Presidential ability, less consideration will be given to the state of origin, the domestic economic policy, the political experience, and even the family life of the aspirants."[8] This is not to say that specific tests of availability will be entirely discarded. Divorced presidential candidates will still find it more difficult than others to win Presidential nominations. Candidates who have never held elective office and with no previous experience in government also will find it hard going to capture the nomination. But these odds, it must be cautioned, are not insurmountable.

In summary, the decline in the importance of "availability" can be related to the expanded power of the Presidency, the growth of new nominating strategies, and changes in electoral politics, especially the "nationalizing" or spread of two-party competition to a majority of states in the Union.

Picking the Presidential Nominee

Even though the interaction of presidential primary victories, public opinion polls, and the mass media is turning national conventions into decision-registering assemblies, instead of deliberative bodies, these powerful influences still have not preempted one aspect of the conventions that never ceases to fascinate the delegates and observers alike: the uncertainty of the outcome. Though the front-runners may have cross-checked their delegate count and tabulated their scorecard totals down to the last confirmed vote, an air of tense uncertainty always hangs over the convention hall throughout the final hours before the formal nomination of candidates and balloting commences.

Rumors sweep through the delegations; the hotel lobbies are filled with talk and gossip about last-minute switches; the television network reporters may even try to generate stories about some eleventh-hour bargaining that may threaten to upset the front-runner's carefully-mapped strategy—all these factors help keep the candidates and delegates on a high emotional pitch as the convention moves toward its climax. The average delegate's lack of confirmatory information and absence of a personal intelligence network—even though he may have heard that the delegate counts compiled by the television network and the wire services show that the front-runner has an insurmountable lead—heightens the uncertainty about the convention's choice for President. This absence of information in the past has sometimes enabled "dark horse" candidates to stampede conventions. Indeed, as long as national conventions are held and as long as the vast majority of delegates are not all bound by mandatory presidential primary laws instructing them to vote for the winner of the primary, the element of uncertainty will continue to pervade the convention hall as the roll call draws near.

Once all the contenders have been nominated, the drama and

suspense of the national convention reaches a peak when the convention chairman declares, "The clerk will read the roll call: . . . Alabama,____votes; Arkansas,____votes. . . ." The balloting is conducted state-by-state by an oral vote. Each state delegation chairman announces the vote of his delegates. Though it has not been necessary to go beyond the first ballot in either party since 1952, successive ballots will be taken until a majority is obtained by one of the candidates. Before the official results of each ballot are announced, state delegations may request the convention to change their vote. One of the most memorable shifts occurred at the 1952 GOP convention when the Minnesota standard was wigwagged to attract Convention Chairman Joseph Martin's attention. Martin recognized the Minnesota delegation chairman, who announced that Minnesota wished to change all of its twenty-eight votes to General Eisenhower. Since Eisenhower had 595 votes and needed only 605 for a majority, the additional nineteen votes in the Minnesota delegation were more than enough votes for the General to win on the final, first-round count.[9] As soon as a candidate goes over the top, pandemonium breaks loose. When the chairman finally restores order (since the advent of television, floor demonstration time has been halved and the Democrats have banned demonstrations in 1972), a spokesman for the leading rival candidate usually moves that the rules be suspended and that the nomination be made unanimous.

As indicated earlier, the potent forces of mass democracy affecting the nominating process now usually single out the pre-convention front-runner for the nomination weeks before the convention opens. This usually means that the nominee is selected on the first ballot. Indeed, both parties have picked the nominee on the first ballot in nine of the last eleven conventions since 1928. This figure may be somewhat misleading; however, since it includes three renominations for Roosevelt, one each for Hoover and Eisenhower, and the nomination of two incumbent Presidents (Truman and Johnson), who had been elevated to the Presidency upon the death of the incumbent (see Table 4.1). With trend toward nomination of the first ballot ballot, the conven-

TABLE 4.1 **Number of Presidential Ballots in National Party Conventions 1928–1968**

YEAR	DEMOCRATS	REPUBLICANS
1928	1	1
1932	4	1*
1936	1*	1
1940	1*	6
1944	1*	1
1948	1*	3
1952	3	1
1956	1	1*
1960	1	1
1964	1*	1
1968	1	1

First Ballot Total   9/11 (5 incumbents)   9/11 (2 incumbents)

First Ballot Nominations: Nonincumbents   11/15
                           Incumbents   7/7
                           * Incumbents renominated

tion's action becomes rather anti-climatic—but one would not think so in viewing the proceedings.

The "nationalizing" forces in American political life also would seem to have ruled out—if the impatience of millions of viewers in the nation's television audience has not—the marathon conventions of yesteryear. In this rapidly-moving age it is sometimes forgotten that in earlier periods of our history thirty to forty ballots (especially at Democratic conventions) were not unusual before a clear-cut winner emerged from the field. In 1880, the Republicans took 35 ballots to select James A. Garfield as its nominee. In 1912, the Democrats could not agree on its winning candidate—Woodrow Wilson—until the 46th ballot. In 1920, it took the Democrats 44 ballots before they settled on Governor James Cox as their standard-bearer.[10] The chief explanation for prolonged balloting at Democratic conventions was, of course, the historic two-thirds rule—a topic that merits brief elaboration.

The Democratic Two-Thirds Rule

For more than a century (1835–1936) the Democratic party—but not the Republicans—adhered to the "two-thirds rule," that is, the requirement that a two-thirds majority of the delegates voting was needed to nominate a presidential candidate. Adopted at the 1835 Democratic convention, the final clause of the formal resolution states "that two-thirds of the whole number of votes of the convention shall be necessary to constitute a choice."[11] This rule was the outgrowth of the first Democratic convention of 1832. Jackson's renomination was assured, but the delegates agreed that a two-thirds majority would be needed to nominate the vice presidential candidate.

From the 1835 convention onward, the two-thirds rule was adopted at each quadriennial convention on motions that were passed by simple majorities. From time to time the two-thirds rule was debated, but as a leading team of scholars has commented: "Over the years it developed its own body of powerful supporters, strongly wedded to states' rights, party federalism, and the Calhoun doctrine of concurrent majorities."[12] Supporters of the two-thirds rule were determined that no candidate would be nominated without the assent—or at least acquiescence—of most major factions within the party.

Twice the two-thirds rule blocked the nomination of candidates who actually had gained a majority of delegate votes. In 1844 Van Buren polled a majority of votes for seven ballots before the Democratic convention switched to James K. Polk. Sixty-six years later, Speaker Champ Clark of Missouri was denied the Democratic nomination in 1912, even though he obtained eleven votes more than a majority of delegate votes from the tenth to sixteenth ballots. The Wilson and Underwood factions, however, refused to buckle under, despite Clark's majority, and thus blocked the Missourian.[13] Eventually, Wilson won the nomination on the forty-sixth ballot.

In the aftermath of the 1924 marathon Democratic convention, further proposals for abolition of the two-thirds rule were heard. Nothing was done about repeal in 1928, however, because Governor Al Smith, one of the losing contenders in 1924, appeared to have the nomination wrapped up before convention time. Four years later, when backers of the front-running contender, Governor Franklin D. Roosevelt of New York, sought to abolish the two-thirds rule, the FDR partisans ran into a hornet's nest of opposition. Roosevelt's managers soon concluded that it would be imprudent to push for abolition of the century-old rule against the heavy odds. Therefore, Roosevelt's campaign manager, James A. Farley, appeared before the rules committee to oppose any change in the convention ground rules.[14] But the Roosevelt supporters did not give up the fight entirely. They persuaded the rules committee to offer the following resolution, which was adopted by a voice vote:

> We recommend to the next National Convention of the party that it shall consider the question of changing the two-thirds rule now required for the nomination of President and Vice President of the United States so as to make the nomination by a majority vote of the delegates to the convention with a further declaration that the convention is to be the sole judge of its own rules.[15]

The famous two-thirds rule was abolished by the 1936 Democratic National Convention that renominated FDR for a second term. With its repeal came a decline in the number of Democratic favorite sons nominated at conventions (see Table 4.2). This is understandable, since previously under the two-thirds rule it was the standard practice of state party organizations to put up favorite son candidates to block the front-running candidate—until major concessions on patronage or issues had been extracted from him. Failing that, the state organization of leaders turned to other more sympathetic candidates.

Repeal of Unit Rule

Some critics of the two-thirds rule believed that another historic voting rule at the Democratic Conventions—the unit rule—should also have been abolished in 1936, when the two-thirds rule was dropped. The unit rule, by which a majority of a state delegation cast all the votes of its delegation (if instructed by its state convention or if the delegation agrees to abide by the rule), was first adopted by the Democratic party in 1836. Though occasionally criticized, it was not repealed until the 1968 Democratic Convention—132 years later.[16]

The chief objection to the unit rule in 1968 was the same as that made in 1936, and earlier: namely, the unit rule, theoretically at least, permitted an embattled convention minority to frustrate the will of the majority whenever it was used. (The GOP, for this reason, has never used the unit rule.) Indeed, under the unit rule prior to repeal of the two-thirds rule, a presidential nomination could have been blocked, theoretically at least, by a cohesive minority faction with considerably less than one-third of the voting strength of the entire convention, if these votes were distributed in such a way as to form working majorities within

TABLE 4.2 **Democratic Favorite Son Candidates Polling 15 Votes or More at National Conventions (first ballot only) When Democrats Have Been the Out-Party or When an "Open" Convention Race Has Existed   (1920–1968)**

1920	11
1924	10
1928	10
1932	6
1952	5
1956	5
1960	3
1968	0

delegations that comprised a total of one-third plus one of the voting delegates of the National Convention.[17]

The unit rule, as explained above, was not imposed upon the states by the Democratic national convention; rather, the convention merely enforced the instructions imposed upon a state delegation by the state party convention. In the case of delegates chosen in presidential primaries, the national convention recognized state laws that excluded these delegates from the operation of the unit rule.[18]

Prior to its repeal, the unit rule had been losing its popularity. Only ten states were bound by the unit rule at the 1964 Democratic Convention. It had been a common assumption that the unit rule was retained, as the two-thirds rule before it, only to placate the Southern Democrats. However, a perusal of the list of the nine states that were still using the unit rule when they arrived at the 1968 Democratic National Convention indicates that while it was used most frequently in the South (Arkansas, Mississippi, South Carolina, and Texas), the other five states that still adhered to the rule (Alaska, Maryland, Massachusetts, Kansas, and Oregon) were scattered across the map.

Vice Presidential Nomination

The last major substantive item of convention business is selecting the Vice Presidential nominee. During the tense prenomination maneuvering and the presidential balloting the delegates are usually so deeply preoccupied with who is to be the nominee that there is scarcely a moment to reflect on the choice for the number two spot on the ticket. Yet, in view of the fact that four Vice Presidents have succeeded to the Presidency upon the death of the incumbent thus far in the twentieth century (Theodore Roosevelt, Coolidge, Truman, and Johnson), the selection of the vice presidential candidate who may unexpectedly be elevated to the Presidency is not a superficial task.

Generally, the choice of the presidential running-mate is held over until the day following the presidential balloting. Meanwhile, it is customary for the nominee to sound out key party leaders on their recommendations for Vice President—even though the nominee may have already made up his mind on his own choice. Indeed, it is now universally accepted that the presidential nominee's choice for running-mate will be approved by the convention by a routine roll-call vote, whether the vice presidential candidate be a popular favorite or a surprise choice. This is the reason why so little formal campaigning is done for the Vice Presidency. As Pomper explains, "public preferences are either unavailable or unsolicited, party leaders have few commitments other than tepid enthusiasm for a favorite son, and strategy to gain the second position is undeveloped."[19]

In the past, balancing the ticket geographically has been an important consideration in both parties: if the GOP presidential nominee was from the East, a Midwesterner or Pacific Coast candidate would likely be selected for the number two spot. Within the Democratic party a Southern or Border State vice presidential candidate has frequently been picked to balance the ticket.[20] Another consideration that is often taken into account by the presidential candidate is to choose a vice presidential candidate from another wing or faction of the party. Occasionally the choice for Vice President may be the result of a trade whereby a rival contender or faction gives its votes to the front-runner in exchange for the "consolation prize." After failure to capture the nomination in three ballots in 1932, and when his drive for the nomination appeared to be losing steam, Franklin D. Roosevelt authorized his managers to offer the Vice Presidency to Speaker John N. Garner of Texas, in return for his Texas and California votes (Garner had won the California primary). The 90 delegate votes from these two states were more than enough to give FDR the two-thirds majority then needed to win the nominaton.[21]

The Democratic nominee in 1956, Adlai Stevenson, tried to inject some "grass-roots" democracy into the vice presidential selection process by requesting that the convention, without any guidance from him, choose his running-mate in an open contest. Senator Estes Kefauver, his chief opponent in the primaries, was nominated by the convention. The Stevenson action, however, did not set a precedent. In 1960 Kennedy and Nixon reverted to the standard practice of the nominee handpicking his own running-mate. Kennedy chose a Southerner, Senate Majority Leader Lyndon B. Johnson of Texas, to help keep most of the Southern states in the Democratic column—a strategy that paid off in November. Nixon, then a resident of California, chose Henry Cabot Lodge of Massachusetts—United States Ambassador to the United Nations, an avowed internationalist with a more liberal viewpoint on domestic issues than Nixon. Four years later, Johnson and Goldwater preferred geographical to doctrinal balance, though Johnson's running-mate, Senator Humphrey of Minnesota, was considerably to the left of the President. Congressman William Miller of New York, Goldwater's vice presidential choice, was a fellow conservative. In 1968 Nixon selected a Border State governor, Spiro Agnew of Maryland—a concession to Southern Republicans who had played a major role in Nixon's nomination. Humphrey, the Democratic nominee, chose a fellow Northern liberal, Senator Edmund Muskie of Maine.

In recent years there has been a notable trend toward the nomination of prominent individuals as running-mates. And as the prestige of the office has grown and its political influence increased, major public figures (frequently leading U.S. Senators) have been willing to accept nomination for Vice President. Formerly, the prestige of the office was so low that offers for the nomination were usually brushed aside by prominent governors and senators. In the past quarter century, however, defeated aspirants for the Presidency have been chosen as the Vice Presidential nominee on three occasions.[22] But there are few convention-watchers who urge that this method become mandatory. Otherwise, this requirement would have made Senator Barry Goldwater Nixon's running-mate in 1960, Senator Robert Taft Eisenhower's Vice President candidate in 1952, Senator Richard Russell of Georgia Truman's running-mate in 1948, and except for a constitutional ban on two members from the same state, Alfred E. Smith of New York Franklin Delano Roosevelt's Vice Presidential nominee in 1932.[23] Clearly, the wide policy differences between these presidential nominees and their mandatory running-mates in these instances would have been too wide for the party to present a united front against the opposition.

Soon after the presidential and vice presidential candidates deliver their acceptance speeches to the emotionally exhausted delegates, the conclave adjourns *sine die,* and the curtain comes down for another four years.

The Convention as a Campaign Rally

The growing role of conventions as a campaign rally mechanism to kick off the general election campaign has not escaped the attention of convention managers and political professionals alike. Prior to 1940, both parties held their conventions before July first. As a rule, another ten days or two weeks elapsed before the candidate was "officially" notified that he had been nominated—even though the entire country had been informed by press and radio (after 1924) about the nominations. Before the emergence of primaries, polls and television as major factors in the nominating process, conventions also served more as deliberative bodies than campaign launchers. During this era the general election campaign extended over a four-month period, marked by the usual summer doldrums. This leisurely pace did not pick up until Labor Day, or shortly thereafter, when the whistle-stopping rail tours got underway.

But since the age of television, especially from 1952 onward, national conventions have become an indispensable rallying mechanism for the party faithful and the mass electorate. With the nationwide television audience numbering upwards to 40 million viewers during prime evening time, the convention managers have come to recognize that conventions offer a priceless opportunity to appeal to millions of potential voters. Not only the party loyalists but the uncommitted independents and even some wavering opposition party members can be reached—and influenced—by the cost-free network telecasts. So important are the conventions as a campaign launching pad that both parties hire professional TV consultants to advise and direct the handling of the televised proceedings in order to achieve maximum impact upon the millions of viewers.

In the 1950's one observer predicted that in twenty years conventions would be held primarily to ratify previous decisions and "to stage a rally for the benefit of the national television audience."[24] This prediction about the growing role of the "campaign rally" function of national conventions has been remarkably accurate. Indeed, in light of the transformation of the presidential nominating process which now finds the out-party's national favorite singled out in the presidential primaries and polls and, in effect, "nominated" before the convention, the campaign rally function of the national convention has assumed crucial importance. Indeed, even if presidential nominations were to be handled through national primaries, and even if party platforms were written by a special team of experts, the need for the campaign rally would still be a vitally important step toward capturing the White House.

In discussing the campaign rally function of conventions, we are not talking merely about the cheerleading atmosphere and delegate euphoria. The authors of the leading study of national conventions have summarized the campaign rally activity as follows: "The conventions have the effect of projecting an image of the parties in their collective, corporate identity. They provide a setting within which the major-party leaders and eventual candidates can be subjected to an intense form of public scrutiny."[25] It is no wonder, then, that the growing campaign rally role for the conventions prompted the same authors to conclude: "Political strategists of both parties have thus been compelled to recognize that the campaign begins at the convention, not afterwards, and that it should therefore be conducted as a major segment of the campaign."[26]

In short, while the convention managers are anxious to send the hundreds of delegates home in a festive mood so that they will work feverishly during the general election campaign, the real target of campaign rally activities is the mass electorate watching the proceedings on television. As Dr. Frank Stanton, President of the Columbia Broadcasting Company, has stated (though not without self-interest):

Television has made the convention more than an organizational device to select candidates and frame a platform. It has become the major forum through which voters all across the land come to know the personality of the party and its leaders, to get a sense of their values, to judge them, their characters and their capacity for leadership.[27]

Television coverage, in turn, has triggered demands for reform of conventions. Network executives have urged that the length of conventions be shortened, from four days to two or three days, that the length of the daily sessions be similarly reduced, especially when there is little conflict over candidacy or platform.[28]

Since the advent of national television, convention rally activities have been altered and streamlined in order to project a more favorable party "image" upon televisionland's millions of viewers. Among the first convention rally casualties has been the long "spontaneous" demonstrations for presidential contenders that take weeks to organize. At first, all leading candidates were urged by the convention managers to restrict the demonstrations to a reasonable length, that is, ten or twelve minutes. In 1968, however, the Democratic National Committee banned all floor demonstrations at the Chicago convention. Though one of the reasons for the ban on demonstrations was to help preserve "law and order" among the badly-divided Democrats, the convention managers were well aware that the national television audiences have grown tired of the "hijinks" and contrived attempts to persuade delegates and the TV audience alike that a specific candidate enjoys massive grass-roots support.

More than a year before the 1972 Democratic National Convention, the national committee's Commission on Rules (O'Hara Commission) voted to ban all floor demonstrations, lengthy speeches, and make the nomination of favorite son candidates all but impossible.[29] These recommendations, which were accepted by the Democratic National Committee, will become the rules of the 1972 convention—unless the convention by a two-thirds vote decides to suspend the rules. Such a reversal, however, seldom happens at national conclaves. The elimination of demonstrations was approved after one O'Hara commission member commented that "the American people seemed to have become estranged from the parties, partly because of 'some of the foolishness' at the conventions."[30]

In light of the recommended "facelifting" for the 1972 Democratic and Republican conventions, this seems an appropriate point for taking a critical look at national conventions—the topic of our next chapter.

THE NATIONAL NOMINATING CONVENTION UNDER ATTACK

5 ★ ★ ★

Because the nominating process occupies such a central position in a party system, it is not strange that the screening process that narrows the choice down to one presidential candidate in each major party should be the object of frequent, vitriolic criticism. Invariably the supporters of defeated presidential candidates are the chief critics. But neutral observers have also found a number of flaws in the national convention system.

Major Arguments Against National Conventions

National conventions have been assailed frequently by critics as "unwieldy, unrepresentative, and irresponsible." Conventions have been criticized because they do not speak for rank-and-file majorities and because the conclaves are "rigged," thus blocking an honest, open vote. This criticism, heard since the Progressive era, echoed across the land once again in the aftermath of the uproarious 1968 Democratic National Convention in Chicago. The vicious encounters between the police and youthful demonstrators—witnessed by millions of television viewers—provoked a torrent of criticism, led by students, journalists, intellectuals, and various minority spokesmen. These critics charged that the conventions were too manipulated by the "pro-establishment" forces, too unresponsive to minority elements—in short that the conventions were "undemocratic" because the true preferences of rank-and-file party members were given little consideration.

Most critics (and many supporters) agree that the conventions are too large—so large, in fact, that it is impossible to conduct the proceedings in a business-like fashion. A large number of political scientists have taken this position for years. In 1950, the

67

Committee on Political Parties of the American Political Science Association declared: "Much better results could be attained with a convention of not more than 500–600 members, composed mostly of delegates elected directly by the party voters on a more representative basis (300–350 members), a substantial number of ex-officio members (the National Committee state party chairman, congressional leaders—probably about 150 altogether), and selected group of prominent party leaders outside the party organization (probably 25)."[1] Most students of politics believe the conventions should be substantially reduced in membership in order to foster a more deliberative environment and diminish the carnival-like atmosphere of the proceedings.

Part of the criticism of the national convention has been directed at the raucousness of the demonstrations. But this criticism is, at best, marginal. As Polsby and Wildavsky have observed, "There is no evidence which would substantiate a claim that the final decision is in some way worse than if demonstrations were banned."[2] Participating in demonstrations enhances the delegates' feeling of self-importance, promotes a closer identification with party goals and fosters a sense of being part of the candidate's team. Pendleton Herring's assessment of the mass demonstration role, made three decades ago, is still valid:

> The value of the convention lies in its permitting the rank-and-file of the party to participate physically and emotionally in a common enterprise. Here they have their chance to meet, to shout together, to feel together. The relationship of follower and leader is seldom an intellectual bond. A common bond of sympathy, a common symbol, is easily grasped and equally binding.[3]

While demonstrations must now be curtailed (or abolished) in order to help retain the attention of the nationwide television audience, this mass participation activity—irrational as it may seem—is an unforgettable experience for most delegates who depart the convention with a sense of party mission that remains with them long after the November ballots have been counted.

National conventions have been likened to a combination of circus, medicine show, and revival meeting. How in the name of common sense, the critics ask, can a meeting of hundreds of delegates, many of whom spend more time frolicking in the convention city than attending the convention sessions, be called a deliberative assembly convened to choose a presidential candidate? Former President Dwight D. Eisenhower, twice nominated by GOP national conventions, has depicted the convention as "a thoroughly disgraceful spectacle which can scarcely fail to appall our own voters and create a shockingly bad image of our country abroad."[4]

Some critics charge that the national conventions are concerned only with picking a "winner," instead of choosing "the best-qualified" candidate. In the past, critics have pointed out that vice presidential nominations have been made too hastily, largely on the basis of political pay-offs, and with little regard to the grave possibility that the man selected may be called upon unexpectedly to assume the Presidency.[5]

More fundamentally, the anti-convention critics assert that all the major decisions on the eventual nominee, the vice-presidential running-mate, and the platform are made by "king-makers" —a handful of professional political leaders in "smoke-filled rooms." Meanwhile, the hundreds of delegates sit by passively, accepting these verdicts with sheep-like docility. Conventions, say the critics, are also too exclusively concerned with making presidential nominations; consequently they do not serve as the national governing organs and deliberative assemblies for the major parties.

Another major argument against the national convention is that the nominating machinery is susceptible to capture by a well-organized, disciplined extremist faction of the party, working behind-the-scenes in the party convention states. This militant minority may select a party nominee who is the darling of the activists, but who enjoys only limited national voter appeal. The takeover of the GOP nominating machinery in 1964 by the conservative Goldwater faction is cited as a classic example. In defying the usual custom of selecting a nominee of moderate views, the right-wing Goldwater faction brought down upon the GOP one of the most crushing general election defeats that the party has ever suffered.

The manner of choosing delegates to the national party convention has come under especially heavy attack since the 1968 Democratic National Convention. Before and during the convention, supporters of Senator Eugene McCarthy charged that they were denied equitable representation in a number of state delegations, despite "grass roots" strength among rank-and-file Democrats and independents, because the party machinery was controlled by the old-line party bosses and regular organization Democrats. The McCarthyites also argued that they were denied fair representation in some presidential primary states, despite Senator McCarthy's overall performance in the primaries.

Leaders in the Democratic party were not unmindful of these charges. Shortly after the November election Democratic National Chairman Fred Harris appointed a special 28-member panel, soon named the McGovern Commission (after its Chairman, Senator George McGovern of South Dakota) and urged them to come up with a list of recommendations for consideration by the 1972 convention. The McGovern Commission's proposed reforms will be analyzed later in the chapter.

The year 1968, however, was not the first time the national convention system has been under fire. Over the years the convention has had far more detractors than defenders.[6] From the early years of the twentieth century, Progressive Republican leaders such as Robert M. LaFollette of Wisconsin and others considered the national conventions to be controlled by a dual oligarchy of political bosses and privilege-seeking business interests. In 1912 the charges of "steal" were heard at the Republican convention when several dozen contested delegates favorable to Theodore Roosevelt were denied seats by the Taft-controlled credentials committee. In the aftermath of the Roosevelt convention walkout the newly-established Progressive party, which he headed, advocated a nationwide presidential primary law to take the power of presidential nominations out of the hands of the party leaders and give it to the rank-and-file voters in each party.

Since then, proposals to replace the convention with a nation-wide presidential primary have been offered from time to time. Three Democrats—the late Senator Estes Kefauver of Tennessee, former Senator Paul Douglas of Illinois, and Senator William Proxmire of Wisconsin—have all introduced legislation to estab-lish a national presidential primary to replace the national con-vention.[7] Until the 1968 convention these proposals received only sporadic attention in the press. Sometimes they were accorded the dignity of a Congressional committee hearing, but then the proposals were left to die in committee at the end of the session.

Proposed National Presidential Primary

The national presidential primary has been the favorite cure-all among party reformers for all of the evils of the national nominating convention system. This remedy, on first glance, is deceptively appealing. Instead of party boss control and decision-making in smoke-filled rooms (allegedly an integral part of the national convention system), the reformers' solution is: "Let the people decide on their favorite presidential candidate in a na-tionwide direct primary election." They point to Gallup polls that have shown over the past two decades that more than two-thirds of the sample favor a national presidential primary. In Septem-ber 1968, for example, the Gallup organization asked 1,507 adults the following question:

It has been suggested that presidential candidates be chosen by the voters in a nationwide primary election instead of by political party conventions as at present. Would you favor or oppose this? [8]

The national results:

Favor	76%
Oppose	13%
No Opinion	11%
	100%

Proposals for a national presidential primary can be divided into two broad categories: (a) a national primary to nominate a presidential candidate in each party to replace the national nominating convention; (b) a national primary that would retain the national nominating convention but provide for the election of pledged delegates within each of the fifty states.

Arguments Against The National Presidential Primary

Some advocates of the national presidential primary, in their unbounded enthusiasm for greater participatory democracy, have conveniently ignored a number of formidable problems that would arise under a nationwide primary.

First of all, a nationwide primary would subject the country to a full year of concentrated campaigning and, quite possibly, three national elections. In an open, free-for-all national presidential primary it is quite likely that as many as eight, ten, or a dozen candidates could be expected to qualify for the race. With a wide open contest it is more than likely that no candidate would receive a majority of votes in the national primary. To avoid a plurality winner, a second or "run-off" primary would be required—just as is done in many southern Democratic gubernatorial and congressional primaries—between the two top vote-getters. The general election, which would probably be the third national election within a nine-month period, might begin to overtax the average citizen's patience with the democratic process.[9] This voter reaction might further reduce voter participation, which now averages only slightly above 60 per cent of the electorate in presidential elections—the lowest among the Western democracies.[10]

Secondly, the cost of financing two national primaries would be almost prohibitive for most candidates. The estimated price tag of all national, state, and local elections for 1968 approached $300 million—perhaps higher. According to Dr. Herbert Alexander, an estimated $45 million was spent in quest of the GOP and Democratic presidential nominations in 1968 (see Table 5.1).

Two more national elections might easily double—perhaps triple—the $45 million figure. Television "spot" announcements, radio time, airline tickets, organization and headquarters costs would probably have to be budgeted for at least a year ahead, instead of the present two-month general election campaign period and the earlier presidential primary campaign season. The task of soliciting campaign funds for three elections would be a mammoth job, requiring a large corps of fund-raisers. Be-

TABLE 5.1 **Estimated Presidential Pre-Nomination Expenditures in 1968**

POLITICAL PARTY	PRESIDENTIAL CANDIDATES	EXPENDITURES
DEMOCRATS	Eugene McCarthy	$11,000,000
	Robert Kennedy	$ 9,000,000
	Humphrey and stand-in candidates in Indiana and California	$ 5,000,000
	George McGovern	$ 74,000
	Lester Maddox	$ 50,000
		$25,124,000
REPUBLICANS	Richard Nixon	$10,000,000
	Nelson Rockefeller	$ 8,000,000
	George Romney	$ 1,500,000
	Ronald Reagan	$ 750,000
	Harold Stassen	$ 90,000
		$20,340,000

Source: Herbert E. Alexander. *Financing the 1968 Election* (Lexington, Mass.: D.C. Heath and Company, 1968), pp. 7–72.

cause it is highly doubtful that candidates of modest means would be able to raise a large war chest, a national primary would restrict the field to wealthy candidates or men who would have their campaigns underwritten by the special interests—unless campaign costs were heavily subsidized by the federal government. One joint-author team has half-jokingly suggested that if a national primary were adopted "the United States might have to restrict its presidential candidates to wealthy athletes."[11] Nor is it entirely a tongue-in-cheek statement to assert that after three elections the winning candidate might be not only totally insolvent but also too exhausted to assume office for several weeks.

Third, a national presidential primary might also lead to a general weakening of the two-party system. Since it is not uncommon for the in-party to remain in office for several terms, a prolonged period of electoral victories for one party might, if state experience with the direct primary has any validity, produce a heavy movement of voters into the primary of the dominant party. The late V. O. Key found that over a period of time the voters in primaries have a tendency to participate in the primary of the dominant party where, they feel, their votes count more.[12] With the desertion of voters from the losing party, only the "true believers" or die-hards would be left. These veteran party holdovers are usually far more interested in nominating candidates whose doctrinal credentials are pure than selecting attractive, middle-of-the-road vote-getters. The end result has usually been that the losing party continues to lose, and party atrophy sets in. If this were to hold true on the national scene, strong two-party competition would be seriously weakened. This, in its turn, might well produce fissures in the dominant party and probably lead to intense factionalism, as has happened in some one-party states in the South and former one-party states of the Midwest.[13] The chaotic disruption caused by two or more major candidates fighting last-ditch battles in two national primary elections cannot be dismissed lightly.

To be successful, candidates would have to build personal campaign machines in most or all of the fifty states, or develop working alliances with the local organizations. After a nation-wide, no-holds-barred fight for the presidential nomination, it is difficult to foresee an easy healing of party wounds. Sidney Hyman, in assessing this prospect, has drawn a gloomy picture of the future: "Instead of the coalitions our parties now seek before they bid for the management of the government, we would have the ideological and fractional parties which lead to coalition governments after elections are held."[14] Gerald Pomper is equally pessimistic: "Rather than promoting democracy, a national presidential primary might impair it, by damaging the unity and effectiveness of the parties. Engaged in a nationwide contest the various factions of the party would draw apart. Repeated contests between the factions might result in the formal separation of the contending groups and the collapse of the two-party system."[15] The concurrent selection of a vice presidential nominee in a national presidential primary could create the additional problem of an unbalanced ticket and give rise to Vice Presidents who would not enjoy the confidence or trust of the President.

Probably the most destructive aspect of the national primary would be its impact upon party unity. Assuming that delegations to the national conventions would be elected in states and assuming that no presidential candidate in a five or ten-man field had a majority, it is extremely difficult to understand how the party could achieve basic agreement on candidates (even with a run-off national primary) and the party platform. The party convention, as Polsby and Wildavsky have pointed out, ". . . aids party unity in a variety of ways. It provides a forum in which initially disunited fragments of the national party can come together and find common ground as well as a common nominee."[16] If a national primary system based upon delegates elected in the individual states were used, final agreement on candidates would probably take as much or more time than the lengthy nineteenth century conclaves. Leading party contenders, lacking a clear majority of delegate votes, would attempt to block or veto rival contenders and perhaps leave the electorate with a choice of unknown candidates whose major qualifications might be the least number of enemies they had made at the convention and during the national primary campaign. Dissension within the party ranks would dominate convention activity. And in the process the electorate would most likely become confused or indifferent about the seeming inability of parties to agree on a nominee or platform.

In reply to the critics of the national convention, Pomper has commented, "Generally, the supposition underlying the proposals for a national primary is that the conventions will reject the most popular and most qualified candidate in favor of some obscure but pliant party professional."[17] However, the experience of the twentieth century, with only a few exceptions, shows that just the opposite has occurred. When a popular favorite has been clearly established in the pre-convention period, the delegates will nominate him with little hesitation.

The proposal for a national presidential primary would saddle the country with a rigid nominating system. The ready flexibility of the national conventions would be lost. Even if a national primary were established by statute rather than by constitutional amendment, a national primary law might mean that the law written to deal with the circumstances in one presidential election year might require major amendments before the next election.

Additionally, the national primary might open the door to demogogues and extremist candidates who, with few ties or strong loyalty to party principles, might seek to stir up mass hatred and hysteria over ideological or racial questions. By making wild, extravagant campaign promises, these demogogues could conceivably make a mockery of the electoral process.[18] In any event, the more extreme factional candidate would lack appeal to the independent and opposition party voters. Under these circumstances the entire nation would be the loser as it suffered the ill effects of two extremist candidates engaged in a fight-to-the-finish.

Finally, many party-watchers believe that a nationwide presidential primary would probably remove any important role the major parties might play in the presidential selection process, eliminating the shaky national party organization, and possibly making it easier for celebrities or demogogues to win the election. Some defenders of the convention system believe that a national presidential primary, by undercutting the national party organization, would make candidates less accountable or responsible, since having gained the nomination without bargaining for support, they would have no organizational commitments to honor or political debts to repay to the individual state party delegations who have previously made nominations possible.

The Case for the National Nominating Convention

1. Defenders of the national convention argue that many of the accusations leveled against the conventions are exaggerated. These spokesmen point to the overall record of these quadriennial conclaves in selecting outstanding leaders—Lincoln, Theodore Roosevelt, Wilson, Franklin D. Roosevelt, and John F. Kennedy. The advocates of the national convention also call attention to some of the highly-qualified nominees who, though nominated, failed to reach the White House—Stephen Douglas, Samuel Tilden, Charles Evans Hughes, Alfred E. Smith, Wendell Willkie, and Adlai E. Stevenson. (The critics argue, of course, that outstanding nominees were selected despite the system, rather than because of the national convention.) When attention is called to some of the inept and uninspiring nominees who became President under the convention system—James Buchanan, Ulysses S. Grant, and Warren G. Harding—the defenders of the convention usually acknowledge the fact that the convention has occasionally come up with an incompetent. But they remind the critic that the convention record, on the whole, has been far above the average. In other words, judge the convention system by the overall quality of the product—the number of outstanding Presidents that it has produced—not the mediocrities it has chosen from time to time. Morcover, convention advocates remind the critics that no system is perfect and that no other system around the world has worked as well in recruiting out-

standing leaders during times of national crisis. As James M. Burns has evaluated the convention: "It has had many triumphs and few failures."[19]

2. Although national parties operating through the national conventions have not always been able to bind all elements of the party into a cohesive team, nevertheless, as one party expert has observed, "the total performance of the national convention as an instrumentality for weaving together the diverse and geographically scattered elements in each party into a national whole constitutes an impressive political achievement."[20] In other words, the national convention choice is usually, though not always, a candidate who represents a negotiated party consensus in most of the fifty states of the Union, instead of merely a wing or faction of the party. In assessing the "brokerage" function (trading and negotiating) of the national convention, Burns and Peltason remind us:

> Those who look aghast at convention horse trades and hijinks often forget that compromise is the very essence of democratic politics.[21]

3. The "openness" of the national nominating convention system allows a wide variety of influences to shape the delegates' choice for the party standard-bearer. Over a span of time that now extends almost a year before the general election, presidential aspirants may compete openly (though they may not have formally announced their candidacies) for the highest office in the land. In this "prenominating" phase of the race, the public can evaluate the performances of the aspirants on nationwide televised news panels, such as "Meet the Press" and "Face the Nation," and also the evening network news programs.

Next, in a score of presidential primary states the rank-and-file voters can personally assess the candidates, while the entire nation watches under a variety of election conditions and shifting sets of competitors for a five-month period from early January to June. After the voters in the presidential primary states have spoken, the national convention delegates are still free to make up their own minds on the "best" candidate for the party to run for President. Also, during the pre-convention period the delegates will have had the opportunity to evaluate the results of national public opinion poll "trial heats." These polls match the major intra-party contenders against one another. A second type of pre-convention poll will match the leading candidates in the out-party against an incumbent President or other prospective contenders of the in-party, especially if the President has hinted early retirement. While many voters may still dismiss polls as unreliable and unscientific, national convention delegates maintain a hawk-like vigilance in charting the popularity ratings of the various party contenders. That both parties since World War II have usually nominated the candidate at the top of the public opinion polls at convention time suggests that the poll results do influence the delegates, though specific confirming data are still lacking.[22]

Whatever the merits or shortcomings of the convention system, it does provide considerable operational flexibility. As Polsby and Wildavsky have noted: "The convention is sufficiently open to excite great national interest but it is not led into perpetual stalemate by pseudo-bargaining in public."[23] In reviewing the overall performance of the national conventions, it will be found that almost all of the convention nominees have been experienced, tested leaders, committed to the values of a representative system. Over and above this, the convention system has made a valuable contribution to political stability by nominating moderates (with a few exceptions), thus assuring the electorate that American party politics at the national level is conducted in the middle latitudes of political debate.[24]

4. In the final analysis, the defenders of the national convention system declare that it should be judged in terms of an alternative system. What other nomination system provides a more satisfactory means to resolve factional differences, competing ambitions, and regional loyalties in selecting a Presidential candidate? Polsby and Wildavsky, for the sake of argument, have posed the question of alternatives—if the convention system were eliminated:

Let us suppose that the smoke-filled room were abolished and
with it all behind-the-scenes negotiations. All parleys would
then be held in public, before the delegates and millions of
television viewers. As a result, the participants would spend
their time scoring points against each other in order to impress
the folks back home. Bargaining would not be taking place
since the participants would not really be communicating with
one another. No compromises would be possible; leaders would
be accused by their followers of selling out to the other side.
Once a stalemate existed, it would be practically impossible to
break, and the party would probably disintegrate into warring
factions.[25]

James M. Burns has also defended the smoke-filled room sessions at the national conventions by pointing out,

The smoke-filled room is essential to the convention for it
serves as the mechanism that allows party leaders to shift their
choices toward a compromise candidate. Without such mechanism there would be eternal deadlock.[26]

Two additional "fringe benefits" of the national convention
(and objections to the national primary system) are that the national convention can both readily handle platform-making and
campaign rally activities—both of which could not be done
easily under a national primary system.

In any assessment of the national convention and its integral
role in the American party system, it should be kept in mind that
we are dealing with a decentralized structure. The national
party in the United States, if we may use the term, is composed
of fifty autonomous state parties, further fragmented into local
party units, over which *no* national party organ has direct or
effective control. Therefore, any convocation of these autonomous units for the purpose of choosing a national political leader
is clearly more like a United Nations conference of independent
sovereign states than a session of a parliamentary body. Indeed
as V. O. Key observed some years ago, "The national convention
represents the solution by American parties of the problem of

uniting scattered points of political leadership in support of candidates for the Presidency and Vice Presidency."[27]

Upon closer examination, it is evident that many of the criticisms of the national nominating convention are directed at the entire decentralized American party system. This type of criticism is fair only if we make the assumption that the national conventions should become the ruling bodies in American parties, with authority to bind state and local parties to decisions made at the national level. This assumption also requires that the party conventions should represent the party voters, instead of the party chieftains and their spear-carriers. These suggested alterations would be appropriate for a highly centralized, "responsible" party system that reflects the mandate of the voters and can enforce party discipline upon recalcitrant party legislators or functionaries. But the model of a centrally-directed party system is not germane to a discussion of a decentralized system.[28]

Advantages of the Present "Hybrid" Nominating System

The present nominating system is, in reality, a "hybrid" or mixed system, which possesses a number of advantages not always fully appreciated by its critics. The national convention still retains the operational flexibility to serve both as a ratifying body or a deliberative assembly for the selection of presidential candidates. If a national favorite is not clearly established in the presidential primaries or polls, and no single presidential contender clearly outdistances his rivals, the national convention appears to be best suited to handle the "brokerage" function of identifying and selecting the candidate most acceptable (or least unacceptable) to the disparate elements within the party. In more than 125 years, American party leaders have uncovered no substitute political agency that can serve as effectively as the convention for a decision-making mechanism to choose national leaders.

In another study the author has listed the chief advantages of the present "hybrid" or mixed system of presidential nominations that consists mainly of delegates chosen either by presiden-

tial primaries or state party conventions.[29] Though not without
shortcomings, the primary-convention-hybrid system retains the
flexibility of the national convention and at the same time injects
some elements of grass roots democracy into the nominating
process. Meanwhile, it avoids the revolutionary changes that a
nationwide presidential primary would probably have upon the
American party system.

The chief arguments in favor of the present hybrid system can
be summarized as follows:

1. It provides an element of *popular democracy* in the nomination process in two-fifths of the states without destroying
   the nominating function of the national convention. It
   makes convention delegates more responsive to popular
   rank-and-file voter sentiments.
2. It provides greater all-round *flexibility* to candidate and the
   voters alike. Candidates are free to enter or avoid primary
   campaigns. States, in turn, can adopt presidential primary
   laws, revise them, or repeal the laws as state political conditions dictate.
3. It puts a weapon *in the hands of the voters* in the presidential primary states. In several of the states, the voters may
   resort to write-in votes to express their support for a particu-
   lar candidate who may be reluctant to run until he sees
   evidence of substantial popular support.
4. It provides a *nationwide forum* to air the public issues and
   test candidates on their campaigning ability. The present
   system furnishes an invaluable measuring stick for comparing candidates' qualifications and exposing weak vote-
   getters.
5. It opens up the *competition* for the Presidency and thereby
   influences candidates who might wish to remain silent
   about their presidential intentions to campaign openly for
   the nomination.[30]

The unsavory aspects of the old straight-party convention system that operated in the states before the direct primary movement makes it unlikely that we will ever return to the former
system. When, from time to time, we start casting about for an

alternate method of nominating presidential candidates, we may discover that the proposed overturning of the present nominating system might have far more frightening consequences than any deficiencies of the existing system.

In light of the 1968 Democratic convention, however, and the serious charges of its unrepresentative delegate selection process and in view of the escalating demands by students and young people for more "participatory democracy" in all aspects of decision-making, it is unlikely that "the same old way of doing things" at national conventions will be the future order of the day. In the final chapter, we will analyze what the reformers have to say about revamping the national convention.

NATIONAL CONVENTION REFORM

6 ★ ★ ★ ★

Political parties, like sensitive antennae, pick up and respond to the sounds and movement around them. When the demands for national convention reform became ever louder in the late 1960's, both major parties—first the Democrats and then the Republicans—responded to the growing pressure to make the giant party conclaves more representative and open to rank-and-file influence.

In the wake of the turmoil at the 1968 Democratic Convention and following the loss of the White House to the GOP, Democratic National Chairman Fred Harris appointed Senator George McGovern of South Dakota, a late-entry contender for the 1968 Democratic nomination, to head a special Democratic National Committee-sponsored Commission on Party Structure and Delegate Selection "to make a comprehensive examination of proposals to reform the national convention system."[1] The Republicans, savoring their 1968 presidential victory, were less hurried about the question of national convention reform. But before the GOP National Committee started preparations for their 1972 conclave, a sub-committee on convention reform made a number of recommendations, some of which were approved at the July 1971 GOP National Committee meeting. The McGovern Commission, however, engaged in more extensive study of convention reform; consequently, more attention in this chapter will be focused on the recommendations of this panel.

McGovern Commission Recommendations

The McGovern Commission was assigned to carry out the Democratic National Convention mandate that ordered the creation of a committee to study the delegate selection process, with the view toward providing more grass-roots participation by rank-and-file party members. During the spring and summer of

1969 the McGovern Commission held a series of hearings in sixteen cities across the land. Party leaders, including Democratic Senators Edward "Ted" Kennedy, Eugene McCarthy, and Edmund Muskie, rank-and-file members, academicians, labor leaders, and spokesmen for the New Democratic Coalition were invited to testify and submit prepared statements on proposed reforms.[2] No aspect of the party machinery escaped the scrutiny of the McGovern Commission. In February 1971, the Democratic National Committee approved without major changes most of the guidelines of the commission.[3]

Among the reccommendations of the 28-member commission (reflecting the influence of Senator Eugene McCarthy's task force report at the 1968 national convention), was the requirement that delegates be selected during the convention year.

The McGovern panel also went on record that henceforth all elements within the state Democratic parties—blacks, women, and young people—were to be accorded a greater opportunity to participate in the delegate-selection process. The Commission also urged the repeal of proxy voting—a device used in convention states by party regulars to thwart reform elements by outvoting the reformers with proxies.

The McGovern Commission adopted the guideline that state parties cannot "instruct" their delegates to support specific candidates. This will make future "favorite son" presidential candidacies unlikely.[4] More recently, the O'Hara Commission on Rules has made the nomination of favorite sons all but impossible for the 1972 Democratic Convention. Delegates will still be free to vote for favorite sons if they wish, but their names will not be placed in nomination unless they can get the written backing of delegates with at least 50 votes, with no more than 20 from any one delegation.[5] In the past, favorite sons have usually drawn all their support from one state. (The O'Hara Commission recommendations adopted in June 1971 will constitute the rules for the 1972 conclave, unless the convention by a two-thirds vote suspends the rules.)

In a related move, the McGovern group recommended that states using party conventions to pick national convention delegates must elect 75 per cent of the delegates to the state conventions from congressional districts or smaller units. In several states this proposal will cut down the influence of party leaders to select a flock of disciplined delegates-at-large who ordinarily vote with the party leadership, not the rank-and-file.

The McGovern Commission, established in response to the charges that party rules for years have been stacked against insurgents, that minority factions have been stifled in their attempts to open up the nominating process to more grass-roots participation, represents the first serious effort by a major party to reform itself.[6] Not since the Report of the Committee on Political Parties (CPP) of the American Political Science Association in 1950 has the country been treated to such a searching analysis of the internal workings of a party. The CPP Report, however, was more deeply concerned with the disciplined "responsible" parties and structural changes in the American parties, for example, the establishment of a party advisory council and biennial conventions.[7] The McGovern Commission, a careful reading of its guidelines will indicate, has been far more interested in making the present internal party machinery more responsive to the will of rank-and-file party members than engaging in a wholesale overhaul of the party system.

One major McGovern Commission proposal—opening up all party activities to 18–20 year-olds and granting them full party membership—has now been fully realized by the ratification of the 26th Amendment in July 1971. Earlier, the United States Supreme Court upheld the 1970 Civil Rights Act, which included an amendment granting voting rights to 18 year-olds.[8] The High Court's decision, however, approved 18 year-old voting in federal elections only. Therefore, in order for 18 year-olds to vote in state elections a federal or state constitutional amendment was necessary.

Needed Reforms

The appointment of the McGovern and O'Hara Commissions was a recognition by the Democratic National Committee that the time to reform the nominating procedures was long past due. In addition to the proposed reforms already discussed, the reform panels made several other recommendations that deserve brief comment.

MORE EQUITABLE REPRESENTATION   One priority reform on which there is consensus is the need to make conventions (and all other party organs) more representative. The apportionment of delegates should no longer be based on the Electoral College principle (two or more votes for each congressman and the state's two U.S. Senators), plus the bonus delegate arrangement. Instead, the principle of "one Republican (or Democrat), one vote" should be the basis of allocating delegate votes. The apportionment system presently used in both parties unduly benefits one-party and small states. In the 1960 conventions, for example, Mississippi had one delegate for about 6,300 Democratic voters in 1956 and one for 4,000 Republican voters. In contrast, a competitive state like New York had one Democratic delegate for 24,000 Democrats and one for 45,500 Republicans voting in 1956. As for small state overrepresentation, Wyoming had one Democratic delegate at the 1968 Democratic National Convention for every 4,036 Democratic voters in the 1964 election, whereas New York, a large two-party competitive state, had one Democratic delegate allocated for every 24,312 Democratic votes cast in 1964. Convention voting representation should be designed to reflect party voter sentiment in the heavily-populated competitive areas of states, not the one-party enclaves or small states. To achieve this kind of representation, the apportionment of delegates should be based on the party vote in each state in the last presidential election.

The most serious effort to revise delegation apportionment was undertaken by the O'Hara Commission on Rules. Recognizing that any plan based exclusively on the "one Democrat, one vote" principle was not saleable to a Democratic National Committee consisting of two members from each of the fifty states, O'Hara's panel arrived at its proposed 1972 delegation figures by giving equal weight to population as reflected in the 1970 census and the average Democratic vote for President in the last three Presidential elections—1960, 1964, and 1968.[9] As mentioned earlier, however, the Democratic National Committee turned aside the O'Hara formula and other proposals for apportionment on a strict population basis or on a straight Democratic vote of a formula computed by counting the Presidential vote 47 per cent and Electoral College vote 53 per cent.

SIZE OF CONVENTION   Almost all convention observers are in agreement that national conventions, especially the Democratic conclaves, are too large. At the 1968 Democratic National Convention in Chicago there were more than 5,500 delegates and alternates, a figure that had nearly doubled in the previous twenty years as pressure has mounted to accord this form of recognition for workers and contributors.

In 1969, Mr. J. Leonard Reinsch, a radio and television official who has helped direct Democratic Conventions since 1944, proposed to the O'Hara Commission on Rules that there be no more than 1500 voting delegates and 500 alternates. To mollify those would-be delegates who would be deprived of a trip to the convention, Mr. Reinsch suggested listing them as honorary delegates in the official program and giving them souvenir convention badges.[10] The broadcasting executive's proposals fell on deaf ears, however, for the number of delegates approved for the 1972 Convention by the O'Hara Commission and the Democratic National Committee has been increased from 2,599 delegates in 1968 to 3,016 delegates, plus an equal number of alternates.

To limit conventions to the five or six hundred delegates recommended by the American Political Science Association would appear to be a utopian hope. Among most convention observers there is agreement, however, that the two parties should set an upper limit of approximately 1500 delegates—a ceiling that the Republicans have adhered to over the years. But the Democrats who appear to be concerned more about "grass roots" representation at their national conventions than manageable size have evinced little interest in restricting the size of their quadriennial extravaganzas. Also, the Democrats appear to view the convention rally function as more important than making the convention into a deliberative body. Nevertheless, as Gerald Pomper has commented, "Limiting the size of the Convention, however, can contribute to more rational decisions within the state delegations and to more careful bargaining between these delegations."[11]

MORE REPRESENTATION FOR YOUNG PEOPLE Future conventions will need to provide greater representation to young people. With the passage of the 26th Amendment granting 18-year olds the right to vote in state as well as federal elections, the distinction between "the senior party" and the Young Democrats and Young Republicans will no longer be acceptable to young people. As a former president of the Young Democratic Clubs of America told the O'Hara Commission at one of its first sessions: "Young people will not accept as their leaders persons appointed by or selected by another other than themselves."[12] Unlike Canadian national conventions that also nominate and elect the national party leader, the Democratic and GOP Conventions have not given special representation to organized or unorganized interest groups. In Canada, for example, the Young Liberal Association, the Canadian University Liberal Federation, and the Young Progressive Conservative Association students are all given representation in both the national conventions and in the national party organization, for example, the National Liberal Federation.[13] At the 1968 Liberal Leadership Convention that selected Pierre Trudeau as the new Prime Minister, an estimated 12 per cent of the 2,396 delegates (or nearly 300 delegates) were under 25 years old.[14] Since young voters in the United States will no longer be satisfied with the patronizing treatment that the senior members of both major parties have accorded them in the past, it can be expected that both major political parties will open their doors to young persons—or face the defection of many young voters to new third or fourth parties.

PROTECTION OF MINORITY RIGHTS Some form of proportional representation must be developed to protect minority rights on state delegations. This would mean that the supporters of a Presidential candidate with less than a majority at any party caucus level—precinct, county or state—would send their share of delegates to the next higher level. Thus, with the majority never able to shut out the minority, a state delegation would arrive at the national convention roughly divided into groups that mirror the relative support of the various presidential contenders within a state.

One effect of this proposed reform would be to prevent the supporters of a Presidential candidate with 60 per cent control of, say, a county convention from electing 100 per cent of the delegates to the states convention, as they can in many states now. Another result would be the abolition of the "winner-take-all" type of primary now in effect in six states—California, Indiana, Maryland, Massachusetts, Oregon, and South Dakota. Under this type of primary, the Presidential candidate with the highest vote, either for his state or in a popularity contest, gets all delegates, no matter how narrow his margin is over the other contenders.

Overhaul of National Committee Representation

Critics of the existing national convention voting structure have also urged an overhaul of the parties' national committees—"executive agents" of the national party between conventions. Within the Democratic party each state, regardless of how large or small, has two members on the national committee. In other words, Delaware and Rhode Island have just as many votes on the committee as New York and California, though the population of the two smallest states is less than 1 million while the number of persons in the two largest states exceeds 40 million. To correct these gross inequities that give the small states a disproportionate voice in the selection of national chairmen and in other party matters, the O'Hara Commission in June 1971 recommended that each state be given one vote on the Democratic National Committee, with the larger states receiving additional votes. But consideration on this explosive matter was postponed.[15] In the past, the Republicans have had their problems, too, with the overrepresentation of the South on the GOP National Committee. As a corrective measure, they sought in 1952 to give greater representation on their national committee to those states with GOP majorities. Beginning with the 1952 Republican National Convention the state chairman was given voting rights on the committee if any one of the following three requirements were met: (1) the state cast its electoral vote for the Republican candidate for President; (2) the state elected a Republican governor; (3) if a state had a combined majority of Republicans in Congress and the U.S. Senate. In 1968, however, the GOP National Convention decided to forego this weighted representation by granting all GOP state chairmen membership on the Republican National Committee.[16]

Do We Need Midterm Conventions?

In 1950, midterm national conventions were also recommended by the Committee on Political Parties.[17] The prevailing view of the Committee was that unless some meeting of the entire party was held more frequently than every four years, policy would come to be dominated by the legislative leaders on Capitol Hill who have not always been representative of the party's total national constituency. In the words of another biennial convention advocate, "A midterm convention would allow the other elements of the party to bring their strength to bear, while also providing a means of revitalizing the national organization."[18] For the out-of-power party a midterm convention, it has been argued, would give the party a special opportunity to publicize itself and its leadership.[19]

On paper, the midterm convention may look good, but the present author does not endorse this proposal for several reasons. The recent experience of the Democrats as the out-party illustrates the problems that might arise with midterm conventions. By mid-1970, for example, at least six unannounced Democratic hopefuls were taking extensive soundings on their chances for 1972. A midterm convention for these candidates would exacerbate candidate rivalries and turn the conclave into a battleground among rival contenders two years before the presidential election. In effect, this would extend the regular prenominating campaign twice as long as at present. The existing nominating system, with its series of presidential primaries, offers each candidate ample opportunity to campaign for party support and to air his views on the issues without two years of direct confrontation with his intra-party rivals. Unlike yesteryear, presidential aspirants can now depend upon television appearances—network news programs, "Meet the Press" panels, late-evening entertainment shows — to publicize their credentials before the primary season opens.

For those midterm convention advocates who fear that the out-of-power party presently lacks a forum to present its case to the American people, one need only recall Senator Edmund Muskie's election-eve televised reply to the GOP and President Nixon's attacks on the Democratic Party in 1970. Democratic leaders in Washington were elated over the highly favorable impact that his "soft-sell" reply had upon millions of network viewers. It is difficult to imagine how a midterm party convention could have gained a better "image" for the Democrats than Muskie's televised message.

While a midterm convention would allow the party the opportunity to update its platform, add new planks, and to discuss broad policy questions, it seems highly doubtful that the "party-in-the-government" wing of the party—the congressmen and U.S. Senators who are responsible for legislating under the separation of powers system—would be willing to be bound by the midterm convention platform. The remarks of the late Senator Thomas Dodd of Connecticut, who spoke out in 1960 against the idea of making the party platform binding on the party's elected officials may be extreme, but they express the views of many Capitol Hill veterans. He declared the "concept that a convention platform is binding on the elected representative in the

Congress is absolutely inimical to our system of government."
Continuing his argument, Dodd asserted that it would be "the
worst betrayal of trust" for a President and Congress "to accept
whole hog the convention platform of a victorious party and to
subordinate the four-year deliberative process of the President
and the Congress to the four-day drafting process of non-elected
members of a party platform committee."[20] Also, it seems highly
unlikely that Presidents who have become "chief legislator" for
their party would be willing to accept sideline coaching from a
midterm convention, consisting largely of non-elected officials,
as they pilot their programs through Congress.

That the campaign rally function of national conventions
would be well-served by a midterm conclave is also question-
able. Part of the drama and excitement of national conventions
derives from the fact that they occur only once in a four-year
period and coincide with the selection of national leadership. A
midterm meeting without a presidential nominating race would
be a dull affair, as most participants who have attended off-year
state party conventions will attest. It takes the nomination of
candidates and a big election battle ahead to get delegates and
party supporters "to rally around the flag."

While a midterm national convention might help strengthen
the national party organization, the cost in terms of the added
intensification of intra-party presidential candidate rivalry and
the extension of the prenominating campaign to a full two years
would not be worth the price.

Final Remarks

In the first major case study of national conventions made in
1952, the joint authors concluded:

> With the advent of television and the powerful personalizing
> effect of its close-up view of actual convention proceedings, we
> are probably at the end of one cycle and the beginning of an-
> other in the development of public opinion on the nominating
> process.[21]

This prediction, now two decades old, was remarkably accurate. But, alas, the authors could not fully anticipate the trend within the out-party of "pre-convention" nominations in which the front-runner in the contested primaries and public opinion polls wraps up the nomination in the out-party weeks before the national convention assembles. For the out-party national conventions are shifting from decision-making bodies to decision-ratifying instruments. As for the in-party controlling the White House the national convention has not been considered a decision-making body by the incumbent President for more than half a century.

For the out-party, it has been the behavior of the candidates toward polls, and the mass media that is transforming the national conventions into candidate-ratifying bodies. Nationwide television coverage, for example, has turned the primaries into "springtime Olympics" that give the early-bird candidate who is willing to meet all challengers in the primaries a head start on free publicity and the creation of a winning "image."

The powerful impact of winning contested primaries, in turn, boosts the candidate's standing in the public opinion polls to a point that uncommitted delegates can be pressured into supporting the early popular favorite, whether he is their personal choice or not. Since the late 1940's the leader of the Gallup Poll in the final two months preceding the national convention has, with one exception (Goldwater in 1964), captured the nomination every time. And even Goldwater was tied with Nixon for the lead in the final "trial heat."[22] As a result of the powerful interaction of polls and primaries, national convention delegates are being forced to make decisions and commitments on their candidate choice much earlier than in the past. As Polsby and Wildavsky have noted, "These early decisions must, perforce, take place at widely separated places on the map, thus enhancing the bargaining power of candidates, who can deal with the party leaders piecemeal under these circumstances, rather than having to face them *en masse* at a convention, where they can wheel and deal with one another."[23]

The successful ability to utilize mass democracy mandates to influence the nominating process in the out-party—as demonstrated by Eisenhower, Kennedy, Nixon, and to a lesser extent, Adlai Stevenson (in 1956) and Barry Goldwater—has required heavy financial outlays, a large personal campaign organization, and a high degree of skill and attractiveness on the campaign trail and over television. If the candidate has an ample supply of these resources, he stands an excellent chance of capturing enough delegates in the primary and party convention states to lock up the nomination long before the opening convention gavel.

Although this new form of political technology seems to be transforming the presidential nominating machinery into a form of *plebiscite,* in which the convention delegates are presented with a *fait accompli* on the choice of nominee, this does not mean that the convention has outlived its usefulness. The national convention must be retained to meet special contingencies. What political instrumentality is better suited than the convention to resolve a threatened deadlock between two or three leading contenders who arrive at the national conclave with approximately an equal number of delegates, and an unwillingness to agree on a compromise nominee? Under these circumstances the national convention can easily revert to its traditional "brokerage" role of negotiating an acceptable compromise nominee—just as the national conventions frequently did in yesteryear.

Looking ahead, there are some telltale indicators that the national convention will not fall into eclipse after all, despite its declining importance in the past two decades. With at least twenty-two states holding presidential primaries in 1972—the highest number since 1924—and with the prospect of five or six Democratic contenders competing in the primaries (plus one or two unannounced candidates, for example Wilbur D. Mills and Edward Kennedy, standing in the wings presumably awaiting a convention deadlock) the Democrats may be forced to turn to the national convention to resolve a possible stalemate among contenders. The odds on one contender sweeping most or even a majority of these primaries—which include contests in all sections of the country—do not seem bright at this writing. And if Gallup and Harris Polls fail to detect a clear-cut favorite among the large field of expected contenders, the uncommitted delegates may decide that they can afford to sit on the fence and wait until they arrive at the national convention to shop around for the candidate that meets their specifications for President.

The national convention system, in any case, possesses a high degree of operational flexibility that provides ample opportunity for a front-runner to build up an insurmountable lead during the pre-convention campaign so that he can take the convention by storm on the first ballot. If no popular favorite emerges from the bruising primary battles, or if no candidate takes a commanding lead in the public opinion polls, the national convention can once again become the deliberative assembly that it was before the pressure of "plebiscitarian democracy" turned it into a decision-registering body.

The main thesis of this study has been that the quadriennial national conventions for the past 135 years have, on the whole, performed their nominating function remarkably well—better than any alternative system could have under the circumstances. As for those who wish to overturn the national convention system and substitute another form of leadership selection, the burden of proof rests on their shoulders.

FOOTNOTES
FOR ALL CHAPTERS

1

1 From "Conventions: Nominations by Rain Dance," by Paul O'Neil, LIFE Magazine, July 5, 1968 (c) 1968 Time, Inc.

2 Paul T. David, Ralph M. Goldman, and Richard C. Bain, *The Politics of National Nominating Conventions* (Washington, D.C.: The Brookings Institution, 1960), p. 17.

3 Frederick W. Dallinger, *Nominations for Elective Office in the United States,* (Cambridge, Mass.: Harvard University Press, 1897), p. 31.

4 *Ibid.,* p. 43.

5 *Ibid.,* p. 31.

6 *Ibid.,* p. 35.

7 David, Goldman, and Bain, *op. cit.,* p. 18.

8 "Origin of the Democratic Convention," *American Historical Magazine and Tennessee Historical Quarterly,* July 1902, pp. 267–273, as quoted by David, Goldman, and Bain, *op. cit.,* p. 18.

9 Eugene H. Roseboom, *A History of Presidential Elections* (New York: The Macmillan Company, 1957), p. 106.

2

1 *New York Times,* July 23, 1971.

2 Paul T. David, Ralph M. Goldman, and Richard C. Bain, *The Politics of National Nomination Conventions* (Washington, D.C.: The Brookings Institution, 1960), p. 410.

3 In 1971, the Republican Convention Reform Committee urged the party to enlarge the four standing committees of the 1972 GOP convention rules, platform, credentials, and arrangements to include on each one man, one woman, one person under 25 and one minority group representative from each state. Also, the Republican National Committee received, without taking any action, a report from its convention reform committee that proposed giving women half the delegate seats at national conventions and allocating to young people and members of minority groups representation proportional to their party participation. *New York Times,* July 24, 1971.

4 David, Goldman, and Bain, *op. cit.,* p. 2.

5 The term "rotten borough," borrowed from British politics, refers to

an election district that has many fewer inhabitants than other election districts with the same voting power. In the nineteenth century one rotten borough in Great Britain along the North Sea was reported to be completely under water at high tide.

6 David, Goldman, and Bain, *op. cit.,* p. 167.

7 *Ibid.*

8 *Ibid.,* pp. 167–168.

9 *Ibid.,* p. 168.

10 *Ibid.,* p. 169.

11 *Detroit Free Press,* August 26, 1968.

12 See below, pp. 84–86.

13 *New York Times,* February 20, 1971.

14 *New York Times,* February 20, 1971.

15 *New York Times,* June 17, 1971.

16 In late September 1971, however, the District of Columbia's Court of Appeals reversed the lower court's decision, thereby reinstating the Democratic National Committee's delegate formula ratio based on a combination 46 percent Democratic presidential vote and 54 percent voter population in allocating national convention votes to state delegations. In January 1972, the United States Supreme Court upheld, without comment, the Democratic National Committee's apportionment formula. *Detroit Free Press,* January 11, 1972.

17 Richard M. Scammon and Ben J. Wattenberg, *The Real Majority* (New York: Coward, McCann and Geoghegan, Inc., 1970), p. 149.

18 The authoritative work on the early period of the presidential primary is Louise Overacker, *The Presidential Primary* (New York: The Macmillan Company, 1926).

19 See James W. Davis, *Presidential Primaries: Road to the White House* (New York: Thomas Y. Crowell Company, 1967), pp. 42–76.

20 *Mandate for Reform:* A Report of the Commission on Party Structure and Delegate Selection to the Democratic National Committee (1970), p. 19.

21 Donald B. Johnson, "Delegate Selection for National Conventions," in Cornelius P. Cotter, ed., *Practical Politics in the United States* (Boston: Allyn and Bacon, Inc., 1968), p. 223.

22 David, Goldman, and Bain, *op. cit.,* p. 339.

23 *Mandate for Reform, op. cit.,* pp. 26–27.

24 *Ibid.,* pp. 28–29.

25 See David, Goldman, and Bain, *op. cit.,* "Women Delegates to National Party Conventions," p. 328, Table 14.1.

26 *Mandate for Reform, op. cit.,* p. 26.

27 M. Ostrogorski, *Democracy and the Party System in the United States* (New York: The Macmillan Company, 1905), pp. 120–121.

28 Donald B. Johnson, *op. cit.,* p. 223.

29 *Ibid.,* pp. 223–224.
30 William Baum, Rene Beauschesne, and Anne Bryant, "The Myth of the Republican Establishment and the Goldwater Nomination in 1964," *The Dalhousie Review,* Vol. 45, p. 482, as quoted by Donald Bruce Johnson, *op. cit.,* p. 224.
31 *Ibid.*
32 See Herbert McClosky, "Consensus and Ideology in American Politics," *American Political Science Review* (June 1964), pp. 361–379; McClosky, Paul Hoffman, and Rosemary O'Hara, "Issue Conflict and Consensus Among Party Leaders and Followers," *American Political Science Review* (June 1960), pp. 406–427.
33 *Ibid.*

1 *Minneapolis Morning Tribune,* July 17, 1964.
2 In recent years both parties have started platform work several weeks before the convention. In 1960, for example, the Democrats held platform hearings in several major cities to gather ideas from all groups, sections, and interests in the Democratic party and the nation. See Richard Taylor, "Pressure Groups and the Democratic Platform: Kennedy in Control" in Paul Tillett (ed.), *Inside Politics: The National Conventions* (Dobbs Ferry, New York: Oceana Publications, Inc., 1962), pp. 84–96.
3 Senator Walsh, famed investigator of the Teapot Dome oil scandals during the Harding Administration, also served as chairman of the marathon, 103-ballot Democratic convention of 1924, which lasted sixteen days (June 24–July 9). See Richard C. Bain, *Convention Decisions and Voting Records* (Washington, D.C.: The Brookings Institution, 1960), pp. 240–241.
4 Polsby and Wildavsky, *Presidential Elections,* 2nd ed. (New York: Charles Scribner's Sons, 1968), p. 96.
5 *New York Times,* August 27, 1968.
6 See below, pp. 59–60, for a more extensive discussion of the unit rule.
7 See below, pp. 57–59, for further discussion of the two-thirds rule.
8 Donald Bruce Johnson, "Delegate Selection for National Conventions," in Cornelius P. Cotter, ed., *Practical Politics in the United States* (Boston: Allyn and Bacon, 1969), p. 221.
9 *New York Times,* August 28, 1968.
10 Richard Taylor, "Pressure Groups and the Democratic Platform: Kennedy in Control," in Paul Tillett, ed., *Inside Politics: The National Conventions, op. cit.,* p. 85.
11 *Ibid.,* p. 84.

12 Unless there are attempts to amend the platform, adoption requires only a single voice. Paul T. David, Ralph M. Goldman, and Richard C. Bain, *Politics of National Nominating Conventions* (Washington, D.C.: The Brookings Institution, 1960), p. 408.

13 Gerald Pomper, *Nominating the President* (Evanston, Illinois: Northwestern University Press, 1963), p. 68.

14 Polsby and Wildavsky, *op. cit.,* p. 252.

15 This analysis relies heavily on Karl O'Lessker, "The National Nominating Conventions," in Cornelius P. Cotter, ed., *Practical Politics in the United States* (Boston: Allyn and Bacon, Inc., 1969), p. 247.

16 The first ballot convention tally showed: Goldwater, 883 votes; Governor William Scranton of Pennsylvania, 214; Governor Nelson Rockefeller of New York, 114; Governor George Romney of Michigan, 41; Senator Margaret Chase Smith of Maine, 27; former Congressman Walter Judd, 21; Senator Hiram Fong of Hawaii, 5; and former Senator Henry Cabot Lodge, 3 votes. *Congressional Quarterly Guide,* 1968 (Washington, D.C.: Congressional Quarterly Service, 1968), p. 9.

17 "Vietnam: The Dissidents Walk the Plank," *Newsweek,* Vol. 72 (September 9, 1968), p. 33.

18 *Ibid.*

19 David, Goldman, and Bain, *The Politics of National Nominating Conventions,* pp. 407–409; Gerald Pomper, "If Elected I Promise: American Party Platforms," *Midwest Journal of Political Science,* Vol. 11 (August, 1967), pp. 318–352.

20 Nelson W. Polsby and Aaron B. Wildavsky, *op. cit.,* p. 72.

21 Gerald Pomper, *op. cit.,* p. 76.

22 *Ibid.,* pp. 76–77.

23 *Ibid.,* p. 69.

24 *Ibid.,* p. 78.

25 David B. Truman, *The Governmental Process* (New York: Alfred A. Knopf, 1951), p. 285.

26 Pomper, "If Elected, I Promise: American Party Platforms," *op. cit.,* p. 321.

27 *Ibid.,* pp. 348–349.

28 *Ibid.,* p. 349.

1 Sidney Hyman, *The American President* (New York: Harper & Brothers, 1954), p. 116.

2 Gerald Pomper, *Nominating the President* (Evanston, Illinois: Northwestern University Press, 1963), p. 129.

3 William G. Carleton, "The Revolution in the Presidential Nominating

Convention," *Political Science Quarterly,* Vol. 72 (June 1957), pp. 224–240.

4 In a June 1971 Democratic presidential "trial" heat Senators Edmund Muskie, Hubert Humphrey, and Edward "Ted" Kennedy met the "80 percent awareness test." All other Democratic hopefuls did not. *Washington Post,* June 4, 1971.

5 Pomper, *op. cit.,* p. 131.

6 James W. Davis, *Presidential Primaries: Road to the White House* (New York: Thomas Y. Crowell Company, 1967), pp. 42–76.

7 Pomper, *op. cit.,* p. 130.

8 *Ibid.,* p. 133.

9 Paul T. David, Malcolm Moos, and Ralph M. Goldman, *Presidential Nomination Politics in 1952* (Baltimore: Johns Hopkins Press, 1954), Vol. 1, pp. 94–96.

10 Richard C. Bain, *Convention Decisions and Voting Records* (Washington, D.C.: The Brookings Institution, 1960), appendix D. This volume is an indispensable tool for voting research on all national conventions from 1832 through 1956.

11 Paul T. David, Ralph M. Goldman, and Richard C. Bain, *The Politics of National Nominating Conventions* (Washington, D.C.: The Brookings Institution, 1960), p. 208.

12 *Ibid.*

13 Richard C. Bain, *op. cit.,* pp. 185–192. According to several contemporary accounts, the Clark leaders may have made a disastrous mistake after New York shifted its entire 90 votes to Clark on the tenth ballot. The Clark strategists, instead of starting the eleventh ballot immediately, permitted a long demonstration on behalf of their candidate. This interlude allowed the Wilson and Underwood leaders to contact their delegates and to urge them to stand firm. *Ibid.,* p. 189.

14 David, Goldman, and Bain, *op. cit.,* p. 211.

15 *Democratic National Convention Proceedings* (1932), p. 140.

16 *New York Times,* August 28, 1968.

17 David, Goldman, and Bain, *op. cit.,* p. 213.

18 V. O. Key, Jr., *Politics, Parties & Pressure Groups,* 5th ed. (New York: Thomas Y. Crowell Company, 1964), p. 428.

19 Pomper, *op. cit.,* p. 155.

20 Since 1932, the Democrats have chosen six Southern or Border State vice presidential candidates: Garner (Texas), 1932 and 1936; Truman (Missouri), 1944; Barkley (Kentucky), 1948; Sparkman (Alabama), 1952; Kefauver (Tennessee), 1956; and Johnson (Texas), 1960.

21 James A. Farley, *Behind the Ballots* (New York: Harcourt Brace and World, Inc., 1938), p. 151.

22 Republican Governor Earl Warren of California in 1948; Democratic U.S. Senators Estes Kefauver in 1956, and Lyndon B. Johnson in 1960.

23 Pomper, *op. cit.,* p. 179.

24 William G. Carleton, *op. cit.,* p. 237.

25 David, Goldman, and Bain, *op. cit.,* p. 495.

26 *Ibid.,* p. 495.

27 Frank Stanton. "The Case for Political Debates on TV," *New York Times Magazine,* January 19, 1964, pp. 16, 68–70.

28 Herbert Waltzer, "In the Magic Lantern: Television Coverage of the 1964 National Conventions," *Public Opinion Quarterly,* Vol. 30 (Spring 1966), pp. 52–53.

29 *New York Times,* June 12, 1971.

30 *Ibid.*

5

1 *Toward a More Responsible Two-Party System* (New York: Rinehart and Company, 1950), p. 38. This report appeared originally in the *American Political Science Review,* Vol. 44 (September, 1950), Supplement.

2 Nelson W. Polsby and Aaron B. Wildavsky, *Presidential Elections,* 2nd ed. (New York: Charles Scribner's Sons, 1968), p. 233.

3 Pendleton Herring, *The Politics of Democracy* (New York: W. W. Norton & Company, Inc., 1940), p. 229.

4 Dwight D. Eisenhower, "Our National Nominating Conventions Are a Disgrace," *Readers' Digest,* Vol. 89 (July 1966) p. 76.

5 Austin Ranney and Willmoore Kendall, *Democracy and the American Party System* (New York: Harcourt, Brace & World, Inc., 1956), p. 315.

6 James Reston, "The Convention System: A Five-Count Indictment," *New York Times Magazine,* July 11, 1948, p. 7.

7 See Estes Kefauver, "Why Not Let the People Elect Our President," *Colliers,* Vol. 131 (January 31, 1953), pp. 34–39; Senator Paul O. Douglas, "Let the People In," *New Republic,* Vol. 126 (March 31, 1952), pp. 14–15; Senator William E. Proxmire, "Appeal for the Vanishing Primary," *New York Times Magazine,* March 27, 1960, pp. 22, 82–83.

8 *Detroit Free Press,* September 22, 1968.

9 James W. Davis, *Presidential Primaries: Road to the White House* (New York: Thomas Y. Crowell Company, 1967), pp. 267–269, contains a summary of the general arguments used against a proposed nationwide presidential primary. For other critical appraisals of the proposed national primary see Sidney Hyman, *op. cit.,* pp. 160–166; David S. Broder, "One Vote Against the Primaries," *New York Times Magazine* (January 31, 1960), pp. 6, 62, 66.

10 See *Report of the President's Commission of Registration and Voting*

Participation (Washington: Government Printing Office, 1963), pp. 8-9.

11 Nelson W. Polsby and Aaron B. Wildavsky, *op. cit.,* p. 229.

12 See V. O. Key, Jr., *American State Politics: An Introduction* (New York: Random House, 1956), Chapter 6.

13 *Ibid.*

14 Sidney Hyman, *The American President* (New York: Harper & Brothers, 1954), p. 165.

15 Gerald Pomper, *Nominating the President* (Evanston, Illinois: Northwestern University Press, 1963), p. 221.

16 Polsby and Wildavsky, *op. cit.,* p. 234.

17 Gerald Pomper, *op. cit.,* p. 230.

18 Polsby and Wildavsky, *op. cit.,* p. 230.

19 James MacGregor Burns, "The Case For the Smoke-filled Room," *New York Times Magazine,* June 15, 1952, p. 26.

20 V. O. Key, *Politics, Parties and Pressure Groups,* 5th ed. (New York: Thomas Y. Crowell Company, 1964), p. 433.

21 James MacGregor Burns and Jack Peltason, *Government by the People,* 4th ed. (Englewood Cliffs, New Jersey: Prentice-Hall, Inc., 1960), p. 364.

22 See James W. Davis, *op. cit.,* Chapter 4.

23 Polsby and Wildavsky, *op. cit.,* p. 242.

24 See Herbert McClosky, "Are Political Conventions Undemocratic?" *The New York Times Magazine* (August 4, 1968), p. 10.

25 From Nelson W. Polsby and Aaron B. Wildavsky, *Presidential Elections,* 2nd ed., copyright 1968 by Charles Scribner's Sons, pp. 232–233, reprinted by permission of the publisher.

26 James MacGregor Burns, *op. cit.,* p. 25.

27 V. O. Key, *Politics, Parties and Pressure Groups,* 5th ed., *op. cit.,* pp. 269–270.

28 This analysis parallels the general assessment of conventions made by Austin Ranney and Willmoore Kendall, *op. cit.,* p. 317.

29 James W. Davis, *op. cit.,* pp. 269–271.

30 From James W. Davis, *Presidential Primaries: Road to the White House,* copyright (c) 1967 Thomas Y. Crowell, Inc., reprinted by permission of the publisher.

1 *New York Times,* February 5, 1969.

2 In early October, 1969, the proposed guidelines of the McGovern Commission were circulated for comment among party leaders and participants of Commission hearings. The final McGovern Commission report was issued in April, 1970. See *New York Times,* April 29, 1970.

For the official report of the McGovern Commission, see the *Mandate for Reform,* Washington, D.C.: Democratic National Committee, April, 1970.

3 *New York Times,* February 20, 1971.
4 For a fuller discussion of favorite son candidacies, see James W. Davis, *Presidential Primaries: Road to the White House* (New York: Thomas Y. Crowell Company), Chapter 6.
5 *New York Times,* June 12, 1971.
6 Senator McGovern, at a January 7, 1971, press conference announced his resignation as chairman of the party's reform commission, clearing the way for his formal announcement of candidacy for the 1972 Democratic presidential nomination on January 18, 1971. Congressman Donald Fraser of Minnesota, a member of the commission, was elevated to the chairmanship.
7 See *Toward a More Responsible Two-Party System* (New York: Rinehart and Company, 1950).
8 *New York Times,* December 21, 1970.
9 *Ibid.,* February 17, 1971.
10 *Ibid.,* September 21, 1969.
11 Gerald Pomper, *Nominating the President* (Evanston, Illinois: Northwestern University Press, 1963), p. 256.
12 *New York Times,* September 21, 1969.
13 R. MacGregor Dawson, *The Government of Canada,* 4th ed. (revised by Norman Ward), (Toronto: University of Toronto Press, 1963), pp. 487–500.
14 C. R. Santos, "Some Collective Characteristics of the Delegates to the 1968 Liberal Party Leadership Convention," *Canadian Journal of Political Science,* Vol. 3 (June 1970), pp. 302–303.
15 *New York Times,* June 12, 1971.
16 See Rule 19, *Rules,* Republican National Convention, Miami Beach, Florida, August 5, 1968. The author is indebted to Mrs. Josephine L. Good, Convention Director, Republican National Committee, for calling his attention to this new rule. Letter to author dated February 16, 1971.
17 *Toward a More Responsible Two-Party System, op. cit.,* p. 5.
18 Gerald Pomper, *op. cit.,* p. 255.
19 Paul T. David, Ralph M. Goldman, and Richard C. Bain, *The Politics of National Nominating Conventions* (Washington, D.C.: The Brookings Institution, 1960), pp. 496–497.
20 Paul T. David, ed., *The Presidential Election and Transition 1960–1961* (Washington, D.C.: The Brookings Institution, 1961), p. 61.
21 Paul T. David, Malcolm Moos, and Ralph M. Goldman, *Presidential Nominating Politics in 1952* (Baltimore: Johns Hopkins Press, 1954), Vol. I, p. 247.

22 James W. Davis, *op. cit.,* p. 94, Table 11.

23 Nelson W. Polsby and Aaron B. Wildavsky, *Presidential Elections,* 2nd ed. (New York: Charles Scribner's Sons, 1968), p. 110.

TOPICS FOR PAPER OR ORAL REPORTS based on material and bibliography in the Politics of Government Series

1 Action and Interaction of Interest Groups upon Each Other
2 The Impact of Interest Groups upon Public Opinion
3 The Influence of Invisible Government
4 Means of Communications and Public Opinion
5 Responsibility of Lobbyists
6 Effective Techniques of Lobbyists
7 Advantages of the National Party Convention
8 Influence of Martin Van Buren on the National Nominating Process
9 Success of the National Nominating Conventions
10 Purpose of the National Party Convention
11 Early Experiments in the National Nominating Process
12 Andrew Jackson and the Nominating Process
13 Proposals for Breaking up the Ghettos
14 The Vast Problems of the Central Cities
15 The Feeling of "Anomie" and its Cause
16 The Influence of 19th Century Immigrants on Municipal Government
17 Problems Created by Ethnics and Blacks in the Inner City
18 Home Rule for Large Cities
19 The Effect of Unionization of City Employees on Local Government
20 Responsibility of State Government for the Cities
21 Fiscal Responsibility of State Governments
22 Advantages of the Corporation
23 The Importance of Bigness in Corporate Enterprise
24 The Meaning of Laissez Faire
25 Significance of the Industrial Revolution
26 The Doctrine of Social Responsibility
27 The Split Atom of Property
28 The Policy of Competition
29 Recognition of the Rights of the Consumer
30 The Making of a Successful Lobbyist
31 Effectiveness of the Business Lobby
32 Labor as an Interest Group

33 Legislative Work of the League of Women Voters
34 New York City as Lobbyist
35 Public Interest Lobbies
36 The Success of Lobbies
37 The Political Process of Government
38 The Power of Occupational Interest Groups
39 The Protection of People in the Cross-fire of Lobbies
40 Proposals for Change of the Welfare System
41 Factors that Contribute to Slum Conditions
42 Changing Economic Life Within the Cities
43 The Problems of Urban Renewals
44 The Conflict of so many Federal Grants
45 Sources of State Revenue
46 Limitation of the Taxing Power of the City
47 Government Regulation of Business
48 Welfare Government
49 The New Deal and Business
50 The War Economy
51 The Anti-Establishment Movement
52 The Beginning of the Party System
53 Masonic Influence in New York
54 The Era of Personal Politics and its Collapse
55 The Emerging Democratic Party 1824–1836
56 The Early Democratic Party in New York State
57 Significance of the Presidential Primaries
58 The McGovern Commission Report on Reforms
59 The Making of the Party Platform
60 The Rights of Stockholders
61 The Demands of Labor
62 New Responsibilities of Business
63 Corporations and Pollution
64 The Problem of the Automobile
65 Business and the Oil Spillage
66 The Formation of Public Policy
67 The Weakness of Interest Groups
68 Functional Representation v. Geographical Representation
69 Proposed Reforms for Lobbying
70 Financial Crises of the Cities
71 Confusion Arising from many Special Governmental Districts
72 The Relations of the Federal Grant-in-Aid System and Levels of Government
73 The Quality of Life in the Big Cities
74 The Model Cities Program
75 Civil Rights and Economic Opportunity

BIBLIOGRAPHY ★

Books

Alexander, Herbert. *Financing the 1968 Election.* Lexington, Massachusetts: D. C. Heath and Company, 1971.

Bain, Richard C. *Convention Decisions and Voting Records.* Washington, D.C.: The Brookings Institution, 1960.

Burns, James MacGregor and Peltason, Jack. *Government by the People,* 4th ed. Englewood Cliffs, N.J.: Prentice-Hall, 1960.

Cotter, Cornelius P. (ed.) *Practical Politics in the United States.* Boston: Allyn and Bacon, 1969.

Dallinger, Frederick W. *Nominations for Elective Office in the United States.* Cambridge, Mass.; Harvard University Press, 1897.

David, Paul T. (ed.) *The Presidential Election and Transition, 1960–1961.* Washington, D.C.: The Brookings Institution, 1961.

David, Paul T., Goldman, Ralph M., and Bain, Richard C. *The Politics of National Nominating Conventions.* Washington, D.C.: The Brookings Institution, 1960.

David, Paul T., Moos, Malcolm, and Goldman, Ralph M. *Presidential Nominating Politics in 1952,* vol. 1. Baltimore: Johns Hopkins Press, 1954.

Davis, James W. *Presidential Primaries: Road to the White House.* New York: Thomas Crowell Company, 1967.

Dawson, R. MacGregor. *The Government of Canada,* 4th edition (revised by Norman Ward). Toronto: University of Toronto Press, 1963.

Farley, James A. *Behind the Ballots.* New York: Alfred A. Knopf, 1938.

Herring, Pendleton. *The Politics of Democracy.* New York: W. W. Norton & Company, Inc., 1940.

Hyman, Sidney. *The American President.* New York: Harper and Brothers, 1954.

Key, V. O., Jr. *Politics, Parties and Pressure Groups,* 5th ed. New York: Thomas Y. Crowell Company, 1964.

Key, V. O., Jr. *American State Politics.* New York: A. A. Knopf, 1956.

Ostrogorski, M. *Democracy and the Party System in the United States: A Study in Extra-Constitutional Government.* New York: The Macmillan Company, 1905.

Overacker, Louise. *The Presidential Primary.* New York: The Macmillan Company, 1926.

Polsby, Nelson W. and Wildavsky, Aaron B. *Presidential Elections,* 2nd ed. New York: Charles Scribner's Sons, 1968.

Pomper, Gerald. *Nominating the President.* Evanston, Illinois: Northwestern University Press, 1963.

Ranney, Austin and Kendall, Willmoore. *Democracy and the American Party System*. New York: Harcourt, Brace, 1956.

Roseboom, Eugene H. *A History of Presidential Elections*. New York: The Macmillan Company, 1957.

Scammon, Richard M. and Wattenberg, Ben J. *The Real Majority*. New York: Coward, McCann & Geoghegan, Inc., 1970.

Tillett, Paul (ed.). *Inside Politics: The National Conventions, 1960*. Dobbs Ferry, New York: Oceana Publications, Inc., 1962.

Toward a More Responsible Two-Party System. New York: Rinehart and Company, 1950.

Truman, David B. *The Governmental Process*. New York: Alfred A. Knopf, 1951.

Articles

Bode, Ken. "Democratic Party Reform in 1972," *New Republic* 165 (July 10, 1971), pp. 19–23.

Broder, David S. "One Vote Against the Primaries," *New York Times Magazine* (January 31, 1960), pp. 6, 62–66.

Burns, James M. "The Case for the Smoke-filled Room," *New York Times Magazine* (June 15, 1952), pp. 9, 24–26.

Carleton, William G. "The Revolution in the Presidential Nominating Convention," *Political Science Quarterly* 72 (June 1957).

Douglas, Paul O. "Let the People In," *New Republic* 126 (March 31, 1952), pp. 14–15.

Eisenhower, Dwight D. "Our National Conventions Are a Disgrace," *Reader's Digest* 89 (July 1966), pp. 76–80.

Johnson, Donald Bruce. "Delegate Selection for National Conventions," in Cornelius P. Cotter (ed.), *Practical Politics in the United States*. Boston. Allyn and Bacon, 1969, pp. 199–238.

Kefauver, Estes. "Why Not Let the People Elect Our President," *Colliers* 131 (January 31, 1953), pp. 34-39.

Knebel, Fletcher. "One Vote for the Convention System," *New York Times Magazine* (August 23,1964), pp. 21, 89–91.

McClosky, Herbert. "Are Political Conventions Undemocratic?" *New York Times Magazine* (August 4, 1968), pp. 10–11, 62–68.

———"Consensus and Ideology in American Politics," *American Political Science Review* 58 (June 1964), pp. 361–379.

McClosky, Hoffman, Paul and O'Hara, Rosemary. "Issue Conflict and Consensus Among Party Leader and Followers," *American Political Science Review* 54 (June 1960), pp. 406–427.

O'Lessker, Karl. "The National Nominating Conventions," in Cornelius P. Cotter (ed.), *Practical Politics in the United States*. Boston: Allyn and Bacon, 1969, pp. 239–276.

O'Neil, Paul. "Conventions: Nominations by Rain Dance," *Life* 65 (July 5, 1968), pp. 19–28.

"Origin of the Democratic Convention," *American Historical Magazine and Tennessee Historical Quarterly* (July 1902), pp. 267–273.

Pomper, Gerald. "If Elected I Promise: American Party Platforms," *Midwest Journal of Political Science* 11 (August 1967), pp. 318–352.

Proxmire, William E. "Appeal for the Vanishing Primary," *New York Times Magazine* (March 27, 1960), pp. 22, 82–83.

Reston, James. "The Convention System: A Five-Count Indictment," *New York Times Magazine* (July 11, 1948), pp. 7, 36–37.

Santos, C. R. "Some Collective Characteristics of the Delegates to the 1968 Liberal Party Leadership's Convention," *Canadian Journal of Political Science* 3 (June 1970), pp. 299–308.

Stanton, Frank. "The Case for Political Debate on TV," *New York Times Magazine* (January 19, 1964), pp. 16, 68–70.

"Vietnam: The Dissidents Walk the Plank," *Newsweek* 72 (September 9, 1968), p. 33.

Waltzer, Herbert. "In the Magic Lantern: Television Coverage of the 1964 National Conventions," *Public Opinion Quarterly* 30 (Spring, 1966), pp. 33–53.

Documents

Mandate for Reform. A Report of the Commission on Party Structure and Delegate Selection to the Democratic National Committee. Washington, D.C.: Democratic National Committee, April 1970.

Report of the President's Commission on Registration and Voting Participation. Washington, D.C. Government Printing Office, November, 1963.

Newspapers

Detroit Free Press
Minneapolis Morning Tribune
New York Times
Washington Post

Reference Service

Congressional Quarterly Guide. Washington D.C.: Congressional Quarterly, Inc. 1968.

INDEX ★